GUILLAUME FAYE

TRUTHS AND TRIBUTES

PIERRE KREBS, ROBERT STEUCKERS
& PIERRE-ÉMILE BLAIRON

GUILLAUME FAYE

TRUTHS & TRIBUTES

ARKTOS
LONDON 2020

ΛRKTOS

Arktos.com fb.com/Arktos arktosmedia arktosjournal

ISBN

978-1-917646-50-5 (Paperback)
978-1-917646-51-2 (Hardback)
978-1-917646-52-9 (Ebook)

Translation

Roger Adwan

Editing

Constantin von Hoffmeister

Layout and Cover

Tor Westman

Cover Art

Éric Heidenkopf

CONTENTS

Foreword to the English Edition

By Jared Taylor

I WRITE THESE WORDS with a deep sense of gratitude: First, to Guillaume Faye and his heroic life of struggle for our people. Second, to the men who have contributed to this collection. And, finally, to Arktos Media for publishing this tribute and for introducing Faye to English-speaking readers. Our heroes are not heroes to the larger public, so it remains to us to erect our own monuments and to mourn our fallen.

This book contains a wealth of information about Guillaume Faye that can be found nowhere else. I first met Faye in 2003, long after his associations with G.R.E.C.E. or his 10-year interlude as the 'Skyman' radio personality. Therefore, it was with the greatest interest that I read Mr. Steuckers' essay, which treats Faye's entire career with great detail and sympathy.

Faye was fortunate to have had a comrade in arms of 40 years so intimately knowledgeable about the many stages of his life. Mr. Steuckers tells us the circumstances and consequences of all his major works—not just the books but also the important magazine articles—and even the currents of thought that influenced Faye and that he himself was influencing. An intellectual history of Guillaume Faye is nothing less than an intellectual history of both the New Right and of the far bolder Dissident Right, of which Faye became an unquestioned leader. Thanks to Mr. Steuckers, I now know, for example, of Faye's prankster persona; when Skyman was off the air, he did such things as stroll the streets of Paris pretending to be a blind man and even once posed as a close friend of newly elected President Bill Clinton, in Paris on a mission to appoint a European representative of the Clinton foreign policy. It gives me great pleasure to imagine Faye doing these things.

Mr. Steuckers also writes of Faye's 'heart-breaking naiveté' and the price he paid for it. The Faye I knew had nothing of the maneuverer in him, only a conviction of the rightness of his cause and a passion to pour out his insights before any audience that would listen. I can easily believe he would come out the loser in any office politics or movement rivalry because for Faye, the movement was not about personal gain. As Mr. Steuckers writes, he devoted is life — he gave his life — for the liberation of Europe and its people. This was his passion, not making a name for himself, climbing a hierarchy, or building an organisation to rule over.

In his own essay, Pierre-Émile Blairon captures another side of Faye when he writes: Faye 'was more than just an intellectual; he also had a sense of theatrics and farce.' Mr. Blairon also writes, 'He was, above all else, a brilliant and passionate orator.' After a good meal and a bottle of wine, Faye's theatrics and farce would delight his companions, but it was at the lectern that he became a force of nature. It was my pleasure and honor to introduce him to American audiences on two occasions, at the American Renaissance conferences of 2006 and 2012. Some English speakers had to struggle with his accent — a hostile critic said it was so thick it could float a cannonball — but his passion filled the room and thrilled his listeners. Even in a language not his own, he was an intense, brilliant, visionary. One man spoke for many when he rose to thank Faye for a speech that 'touched my genes.'

No one, whether reading Faye or listening to him speak, could help but be swept up by his conviction, his eloquence, and his sense of tragedy. Faye coined several neologisms and one that will certainly endure is 'ethnomasochism,' which captures the horror of a great people — his people — turning on itself in a frenzy of disgust and contempt. As Pierre Krebs writes in his contribution to this volume, Europeans are 'in a state of war against an enemy that threatens to smother the very Essence of our Being, to snuff out our inalienable right to be and remain ourselves, in line with our ancestors,' but the true abomination is that 'Europe is giving its wealth away so as to fund its own suicide.' Faye was one of the first to see this, to be horrified by it, and to struggle in every possible way to shake, shock, persuade, and shame Europeans out of their potentially fatal ethnomasochism.

It was this passion that drew me to Faye when we met for the first time. After 15 minutes it was clear that this was a man who lived his convictions, and his convictions mirrored my own. Although I was an American and therefore citizen of a country he had often called a competitor and even a rival, he quickly saw in me a fellow European, his own flesh and blood, an ally in the struggle. Perhaps I flatter myself, but I think I helped him see that there was more to America than General Motors, the New York Times, the Baptist Church, and the State Department, that even in decadent America there were men and women who know that our civilisation is dying and are fighting to save it. And so it was that at the 2012 American Renaissance conference, Guillaume Faye, in full sincerity, could deliver a speech with the title: 'America and Europe: Brothers in Arms.' There are a true Europe and a true America, unrepresented in the halls of power, and we are truly allies.

By the end of his life, by the time he wrote *Ethnic Apocalypse*, Faye had no illusions about what was at stake. His last book is a grim warning to the West of what we face and the choices we must make. If all his previous work was diagnosis — brilliant, witty, irrefutable — *Ethnic Apocalypse* is cure. You may have been innocent before you read this book; afterwards, you are innocent no longer. No one who reads *Ethnic Apocalypse* in earnest can escape its deadly logic or remain deaf to its call, a call that rings out to every land where the sons and daughters of Europe have spread the civilisation of their ancestors.

There is little I can add to the esteem and affection for Guillaume Faye that shines through the following pages. The men who have contributed to this book served with Faye in the same regiments, fought in the same battles, bear the same scars. Alas, Faye fell before his time, but he was fighting to the end, writing and thinking even on his sickbed, unwilling to die without a final blast against the forces arrayed against everything dear to him. This book is a heartfelt tribute to a man we loved and admired, but our best tribute is to stay in the fight — Faye's fight, our fight, Europe's fight — and battle to the end just as he did.

JARED TAYLOR,
Oakton, Virginia, USA,
May 17, 2020

Incipit: All Grandeur Lies in the Attacks One Launches

Dedicated to Guillaume Faye

Towers of an immemorial Europe stemming from our most distant days,
from the farthest reaches of our unfailing memory's herculeanly fearless ways,
mastering the energies of which our peoples were begotten,
yet have now been all but forgotten.
Towers which, from our recent deceiving words, do rise
And are brought forth by our surrender and weakest vice,
muting our century's most pernicious lies.

These tall, firm and thick towers
are the citadels of this imperial Europe of ours —
the belligerent architecture of ideological defiance,
the perennial framework of historical reliance.
These deep-rooted citadels are heavy and massive at the base,
all threats and dangers to erase.
High and sharp are their edges, as if those of the reclaimed blades
of our reconstituted phalanxes, defying Europe's divine renegades.

Citadels rising above the desperate fate of our Western Land,
To re-instil faith in the gods' rebirth, now at hand,
The barbaric will of super-humanist challenges heedfully to command.

Though Pericles and Faust may stagger under the diabolically entangled
chains of weakness, shame and betrayal with which they are shackled,
the citadels of Europe remain unshakeable,
secure, strong and impregnable.

A Titan shall be reborn, reborn he shall be,
to shatter the Chaldean fetters and henceforth be free
of the very chains that have kept our souls ever exiled,
our bodies disfigured, our minds miscegenated and defiled.
A Parsifal of the Heideggerian ages leading up to an event,
a development that, to synthesise, is meant —
immemorial pagan pre-science with Nietzschean aeons of advent.

For as the world's clock now strikes midnight,
it is from within the shadows of the fossilised stone eagles
perched upon the towers of our enslaved and enfeebled
fatherlands that the eagle-like might
of our empire-founding energies
and wills is already taking flight,
reinventing our deities.

Written by PIERRE KREBS in the 1980's

I

Guillaume Faye's Contribution to the 'New Right' and a Brief History of His Ejection

By Robert Steuckers

I

UILLAUME FAYE was truly the driving force behind G.R.E.C.E.,[1] the 'New Right's main organisation in France during the early 1980s. Driven by his incredible dynamism, an unrivalled enthusiasm within this environment, his overflowing vitality and a discourse that comprised astonishing and highly appealing moments of sheer brilliance, Guillaume Faye had, as he himself liked to say, been very impressed by his readings of the situationist texts of Guy Debord's[2] school. If we were to oversimplify or strive to summarise the essential/existential core of his approach, we could say that he denounced the ideological stagnation in the aftermath of 1968, that of the 1970s and the Giscard era in France, which he regarded as a stupid, dreary and bland 'spectacle'. Faye was a man who entered the scene virtually alone, at some time between the departure of the partisans of the 1968 events and the arrival of the Reaganian 'yuppies'.

In the second issue of *Élements* magazine, which was, and remains, at the forefront of the oldest cenacle of the 'New Right' in France, whose members gather around the irremovable Alain de Benoist, one can see a photo of the young Faye, aged twenty-three, at a time when

---

1   TN: *Groupement de recherche et d'études pour la civilisation européenne*, i.e. the 'Research and Study Group for the European Civilisation'.

2   TN: In addition to having been a member of the Letterist International collective of radical artists and cultural theorists, the founder of a Letterist faction, and a founding member of the Situationist International organisation of social revolutionaries, Guy Louis Debord (28th December, 1931–30th November, 1994) was a French Marxist theorist, philosopher and filmmaker.

he was involved in the teaching profession as part of the 'Vilfredo Pareto Circle'. In his scientific work *On the New Right*, Pierre-André Taguieff sketches a brief history of this 'Vilfredo Pareto Circle' (p. 183), run by Jean-Yves Le Gallou, a man who is now active as an MEP for Jean-Marie Le Pen's *Front National* party. In 1970, G.R.E.C.E. established its 'Paris-Île-de-France Regional Unit' (URPIF), with the 'Vilfredo Pareto Circle' acting as the latter's branch within the 'Institute of Political Studies' (IEP) in Paris. Taguieff adds that it was, in fact, Faye himself who chaired this Pareto Circle from 1971 to 1973 (Op. cit., p. 205). This being his very first appointment, Faye was thus immediately someone new, someone who was not attached to any branch of the conventional French Right.

He had no ties to any Vichy or collaborationist circles, nor to those of the OAS[3] or the 'Catholic-traditionalist' movement. He was not a nationalist per se, but a disciple of Julien Freund, Carl Schmitt (of whom he had already spoken with simplicity, conciseness and accuracy in the columns of *Cahiers du Cercle Vilfredo Pareto*[4]), François Perroux, etc. One could say that, if such language had any meaning in the final instance, then Faye was, within G.R.E.C.E., the representative of a 'Right' that lay beyond the factions, of a 'regalian Right' that cast upon all events a sovereign and detached eye, which was not, however, devoid of ardour and 'plastic' will, sorting out in some way the wheat from the chaff, the political from the impolitic. Those who kept company with him or, like me, were once his colleagues know that he always made fun of the flaws of those Parisian rightist movements, the stilted attitudes and the prestige-seeking quarrels of those who, in all earnestness and in a display of great arrogance, advocated certain

---

3   TN: The OAS (*Organisation Armée Secrète* or 'Secret Army Organisation') was a short-lived right-oriented French paramilitary organisation active during the Algerian War of 1954–1962 and responsible for carrying out various terrorist attacks in its efforts to avert Algeria's independence.

4   TN: Notebooks of the Vilfredo Pareto Circle.

simplistic ideas: the latter were sometimes Nazi psychobabble[5] of immeasurable inanity, one that was modelled on the ideas of American
comic strips, simplistic notions that obviously bore no connection
to any historical context and failed to mould themselves in a manner that reflected reality. He also mocked — and not without malice,
one might add — all those who, within our world, where so many
psychopaths jostle one another, bestowed upon themselves a 'sublime'
(and often tough and 'supermanistic') character, one which did not
correspond at all to their actual and oftentimes glaring mediocrity.
Faced with all kinds of nostalgia, Faye liked to say that he was both
'realistic and accepting' and that the latter attitude was, in the long
run, the only fruitful one. Indeed, no sooner did the development of
the New Right — either as a metapolitical working network or a specific political commitment to the RPR,[6] the National Front or various
national-revolutionary groups — require rigour and endurance than
the 'supermanistic' mythomaniacs melted away like snow in the sun
or were recycled into small groups in which masquerades and psycho-
dramas were constantly on the agenda.

Faye produced his work in an environment that was not his own,
one that did not fully identify — or perhaps not at all — with what
he wrote. He gave the impression of repeatedly targeting the anthill
with the heftiest kicks, trying to shock people in the hope that this
mischievous maieutic would hatch a truly new 'Right', one which
would not content itself with hastily camouflaging its pro-Vichy attitude, its colonial nationalism, its Parisian lounge-lizard Nazism, its
purely material ambitions or its caricatural militarism under a few
scholarly references. It was ultimately Faye who alone embodied the
'New Right', for never had he been anything else. Almost everyone

---

5   TN: The French neologism 'Nazisteries' has no real equivalent in English.
      Possible translations include 'Nazi psychobabble' and 'Nazi nonsense', though
      these are not the only options.

6   TN: The Rally for the Republic (*Rassemblement pour la République*) was a con-
      servative Gaullist political party.

who was part of his entourage during his passage through G.R.E.C.E. (and thus benefited from his charisma, energy, quick-paced and ever relevant work, and brilliant intelligence) considered him a stranger in the end, a 'little newcomer', who was not to be let in on things and was removed from the movement's actual command centres, where a few 'elders' made decisions that were unappealable and final. From the very outset, Faye would be free of the 'rightist' cangue, which could not be said of his associates and especially those who paid him (so very badly). Naive and ever anxious to do as much work as possible, Faye never cared much about all those vicious backstage intrigues; to him, what mattered was that texts were being published and books and brochures spread to the public. In the end, his realisation of how harmful this opacity was would come too late, with the latter having weakened and handicapped the movement, to which he sacrificed the best years of his life, and enabled endless manipulations and hedging, as he himself ended up falling prey to the plotters lurking behind the scenes, without ever succeeding in patiently building up an alternative apparatus. Faye was indeed a victim of his own confidence, naivety and lack of belonging to a very specific network of the 'old Right', which was basically reluctant to renew itself and face both the world and life head on. Parisian illusions, fantasies, cronyism and intrigues took constant precedence over the ideological relevance of the actual discourse and over all efforts to expand and deepen the movement.

As the 'New Right' emerged, finding itself in the limelight after the summer of the 1979 press campaign, Faye volunteered to go on a continual 'Tour de France' of the regional units of G.R.E.C.E., which were springing up everywhere in a spontaneous manner. Thanks to his personal commitment, presence, and a skilful language that excited people's wills, he turned G.R.E.C.E. into a genuine community in which the 'elders' (who stemmed from all walks of the 'Right', with the sole exception of fundamentalist and moderate Catholics) rubbed shoulders with 'new' people, who were often students and instinctively grasped and accepted the novelty of his speech and the essential notions it conveyed. Highly attentive to the sociological analyses that investigated fashion, examined mores and harnessed the sources of protest as soon as they hatched, Faye became quite naturally the idol of the young non-conformists belonging to the French 'Right', who would soon be joined by some differentialist supporters of the 1968 movement (inspired by Robert Jaulin, Henri Lefebvre, Michel Maffesoli, and the defenders of the Third World against Western capitalist 'homologation') and former situationists who rejected certain classic social conventions (such as religion) without, however, accepting the temptations arising from the implicit ideology of the baba-cools of 1968, which acted as the matrix of the conformism that plagues us today.

Unlike Marcuse's[7] readers, who had bet on some kind of soft *Epimetheism*,[8] an Orphic sort of eroticism that served as the basis of an almost paradisiacal anti-civilisation, a soft and resignation-based type of protest, and a permanent negation of all institutions involving any sort of 'you must' attitude, Faye merged protest with affirmation and rejected as vain, impolitic and capitulationist any and all Marcuse-style opposition, betting instead on hard-line Prometheism; on a goliardic[9] sort of eroticism, which, by spreading healthy joy, promptly frees its followers from the bitter tensions of permanent action; and on a permanent and unruffled affirmation of new duties and institutions, which are, however, not considered definitive. Although Marcuse and Faye both challenge our stagnant society and the old hierarchies of the 1950s and 1960s, what Marcuse attempts to do is exit history once and

---

7   TN: Herbert Marcuse (19th July, 1898–29th July, 1979) was a German-American philosopher, sociologist, and Marxist political theorist associated with the Frankfurt School of Critical Theory.

8   TN: In Greek mythology, Epimetheus was the brother of Prometheus. His name is derived from a Greek word meaning 'afterthought' and contrasting with his brother's name, Prometheus, which means 'forethought'. Epimetheus thus came across as a fool, with his brother being the wiser one.

9   TN: Involving a celebration of licentiousness and drinking.

for all, blaming the latter for having generated these inert hierarchies. As for Faye, what he desires is a return to the turmoil of history while simultaneously believing in the antagonistic and tragic framework of life (just like his mentors, namely Freund, Monnerot and Maffesoli). Convinced of his own anti-totalitarianism, Marcuse actually has a demobilising effect. In an effort to evade the soft kind of totalitarianism that smothers souls and peoples through the limitless extension of its scolding moralism (just as the mind-numbing hierarchism of pre-68 conventions stifled people's creative spontaneities), Faye is, by contrast, hyper-mobilising.

This antagonistic and affirmative vision would thus be conveyed from city to city for several years, between 1979 and 1984, a space-time context in which G.R.E.C.E. was at its height. All of this took place, of course, under the leadership of Alain de Benoist, but thanks to Guillaume Faye's charisma above anything else. The latter left his mark on *Éléments* magazine, defining the topics and approaching them with a passion and timeliness that would never be seen again after his departure. With Faye now gone, followed by Vial and Mabire (both of whom were, however, very different from him), *Éléments* began to literally flounder; the magazine lost its 'core' and became an arena where very young polygraphs, mediocre paraphrasers and incorrigible compilers, fake Germanists and false philosophers, false leftists and fake neo-fascists, scribblers of ephemerides and dreary aesthetes all amused themselves, not to mention, above all, some fine samples of 'slap-worthy' individuals from the sixteenth arrondissement. It was, in fact, Faye who launched many new topics that were mostly unknown among the ranks of the 'stupidest Right in the world'. Thanks to his effortless contact with academics (unlike Alain de Benoist), what Faye grafted on his initial legacy of political sciences and the Pareto Circle was novelty, introducing his own interpretation of Habermas' 'communicative action', the theories of American neoconservatives and Christopher Lash's anti-narcissistic sociology. Then, breaking resolutely with right-wing 'Westernism', Faye initiated, in the 32nd issue of *Éléments*, his own criticism of Western civilisation, establishing or renewing a connection not only with the anti-Westernism of the German nationalists or conservatives of the Weimar era (including Spengler, Niekisch, Sombart, etc.)', but also with the ethnological arguments that stigmatised the 'ethnocides' occurring on the fringes of the West's techno-messianic civilisation (Robert Jaulin) and with the *Differentialist Manifesto* penned by Henri Lefèbvre (a former French Communist Party theorist who was also once a disciple of surrealist André Breton). Westernism, heir to a stagnant, fixist, immobilist, humanitarian, repetitive, and parrot-like conception of the Enlightenment, is a cangue from which one must free oneself, as it impedes 'communicative action' (which the young Habermas had dreamt of and Faye and his true friends would long to restore in their community-related, identitarian and deep-rooted logic). It is a pathological state that generates false and ineffective hierarchies, which a rotation of elites will have to bring down. Last but not least, and in accordance with Faye's brilliant formula, it acts as a 'system for killing peoples'.

And yet, although the criticisms formulated by the proponents of the Frankfurt School and by Faye himself both reject the system founded by the ideology of the Enlightenment (since this system obliterates Life, meaning our *Lebenswelt*, a term adopted by Habermas and previously used by Simmel), these two schools — namely the New Left, whose best platform is epitomised by the New York-based magazine *Telos*, and the real New Right, which Faye was alone to embody, without ever finding himself entangled in incapacitating bouts of nostalgism — differ in their appreciation of 'instrumental reason'. In the eyes of the Frankfurt School, instrumental rationality is the source of all ills: from Manchesterian capitalism to the authoritarianism of the *Obrigkeitsstaat*, from fascism to the abandonment of the famous *Lebenswelt*, and from electro-fascism (Jungk) to the destruction of the environment. From Faye's perspective, however, instrumental reason is a source of power, and it takes power to make things happen in politics, including the fact of restoring our *Lebenswelt,* our roots and our people's spontaneity. The difference between the New Right (i.e. Faye) and the New Left (the *Telos* team, basically) is to be sought entirely in this issue of power, in connection to which instrumental reason can serve as a tool. This dispute was also that of German social sciences (See *De Vienne à Francfort, la querelle allemande des sciences sociales,*[10] Ed. Complexe, Brussels, 1979): is it instrumental reason, which puts values in brackets, makes no value judgments and practices the *Wertfreiheit* postulated by Max Weber or perhaps even the ethics of responsibility, that is to gain the upper hand? Or is it, in fact, normative reason, which insists on values (albeit only the 'enlightened' values of the modern West) and thus develops an ethics of conviction, that should come out on top? Although Faye never answered this exact question within the framework of the debate that shook the intellectual world at the end of the 1970s and the beginning of the 1980s, one perfectly sensed, both in his articles and his 'System for Killing Peoples',[11] that he intuitively perceived the hiatus or perhaps even impasse: indeed, he knew that both instrumental reason (when handled by political authorities that do not share our values, i.e. those of the Greek *zoonpolitikon* or Roman hyper-politics, nor, above all, our metaphysical and legal traditions) and normative reason (whenever it proceeds to impose abstract or foreign norms on our history) can be obliterating and alienating. And although it would be more accurate to speak of 'axiological reason' instead of a normative one, in the sense that a 'norm', as defined by Carl Schmitt, is always an abstraction that latches itself onto life, whereas a value, as understood by Weber and Freund, is an immutable positivity that can undergo a change of form but never one of content and, while remaining the prerogative of specific cultures or peoples, burst into reality, withdraw from it or enter a state of latency, neither reason is actually obliterating nor alienating

---

10   TN: From Vienna to Frankfurt, the German Social Sciences Dispute.

11   TN: Published in French as '*Le système à tuer les peuples*'.

as long as peoples live by their own values and are not subjected to abstract standards that deliberately eradicate all that is spontaneous, correcting whatever seems irrational to them and erasing historical legacies.

Faye did not have the necessary time to become involved in the debates that raged around Rawls' work (on social justice), nor the time to follow the debates promoted by American 'communitarians', who have found their cementing values within the field of sociology and intend to reactivate them. And above all, he did not keep track of the great secret adventure of the 1980s, namely the rediscovery of Carl Schmitt's work in Germany, Italy and the United States, with France remaining more or less outside this groundswell, which spanned across the entire planet. One only finds themselves outside the dilemma between instrumental reason and normative reason if one turns to history, which offers specific values for specific peoples, values that are perhaps fundamentally subjective yet *also* objective, as they are the only ones capable of structuring coherent and lasting behaviours within a context of flexibility and generating, within a given people, what Arnold Gehlen[12] termed 'institutions'. A people who adhere to and put into practice their own values obey laws which are objective to them alone, but which are the only practical objectivity in the political sphere; if they obey norms that are extrinsic to them, imposed by external and/or dominant powers, normative reason will, whether consciously or unconsciously, seem alienating to them, and instrumental reason unbearable. In such a context, the people in question will die if they have forgotten their own values, because they can no longer act according to their own internal laws. And it is the system that will have killed them.

Indisputable and determining was the influence of Henri Lefebvre on the evolution of Guillaume Faye's ideas; Henri Lefebvre was one of the main theorists of the French Communist Party and the author of

---

12   TN: Arnold Gehlen was a prominent conservative German philosopher, sociologist, and anthropologist.

many fundamental texts intended to be used by the militants of this highly organised and combative party. Guillaume Faye and I had the pleasure of meeting this ex-communist French philosopher on two occasions in the hall of the famous Parisian restaurant 'La Closerie des Lilas', which Lefebvre liked to frequent because it had once been an important venue from the Parisian surrealist perspective, back in the days of André Breton. Lefebvre liked to recall the Homeric rows between the surrealists and their adversaries, rows that had enlivened the restaurant. Before embracing Marxism, Lefebvre had been a surrealist. The conversations we had with this philosopher of exceptional distinction, who was highly refined and very aristocratic in his words and manners, were fruitful and contributed, in particular, to enriching the *Nouvelle école* issue that focused on Heidegger and which we were preparing at the time. Three additional and recent works by Lefebvre, all of which were post-Marxist, caught our attention: *Position: contre les technocrates. En finir avec l'humanité-fiction*[13] (Gonthier, Paris, 1967); *Le manifeste différentialiste*[14] (Gallimard, Paris, 1970); and *De L'État. 1. L'État dans le monde moderne*,[15] (UGE, Paris, 1976).

In *Position* (op. Cit.), Lefebvre protested against both space and lunar exploration projects because they turned man away from 'the humble surface of the globe', causing him to lose his sense of Earth, which was so dear to Nietzsche. In Lefebvre's eyes, it was also the result of an ideology that had lost all practical potential and any ability to forge a specific project that would remedy the issues that affect the real lives of men and cities.

This ideology, which is that of 'liberal bourgeois humanism', is no more than a 'mixture of philanthropy, culture and citations'; within it, philosophy is ritualised, becoming a mere ceremonial system that sanctions an extensive fool's game. From Lefebvre's perspective, such

---

13　TN: Position: Against Technocrats — Doing Away with a Fictitious Humanity.

14　TN: The Differentialist Manifesto.

15　TN: On the State volume 1: The State in the Modern World.

stagnation in pure phraseology should not lead us to reject man as the structuralists around Foucault do, casting destructive and 'deconstructivist' suspicion upon all political projects and wills (though, at a later point, Lefebvre would no longer be so severe towards Foucault). In such a context, no further revolutionary impetus — or of any other kind — is possible: movement, dialectic, dynamics and becoming are all simply denied. Anti-historicist and Foucauldian structuralism is the peak of the rejection that targets the formidable potential that Heraclitus bequeathed to us, ushering in, says Lefebvre, a new 'Eleaticism': whereas the old Eleaticism challenged sensory movement, the new one denounces historical movement. To Lefebvre, Parmenidean philosophy is one of immobility. To Faye, the neo-Parmenidean attitude espoused by the liberal, bourgeois and plutocratic system is the philosophy of the liberal-humanist discourse that is endlessly repeated as a dry sort of catechism devoid of any marvellous aspects. In Lefebvre's eyes, Heraclitean philosophy is the philosophy of movement. To Faye, who thus displays some Spenglerian echoes specific to the neo-rightist takeover of the Weimarian 'Conservative Revolution' (through Locchi and de Benoist), contemporary Heraclitism must be a joyful cult of innovative mobility. To both Lefebvre, the ex-Marxist and ex-surrealist, and the absolute neo-rightist that Faye was, beings, stabilities and structures are mere traces of the journey of Becoming. In their eyes, there are no static and definitive structures: the real movement characterising both the world and politics is a movement subject to constant structuring and de-structuring. The world cannot be locked into a system whose sole concern is to preserve itself. One must counter this structuralism, which can justify systems through the exclusion of the 'anthropos' of flesh and willpower, with an anti-system or even with Life itself. From Lefebvre's (and Faye's) perspective, this recourse to Life is not synonymous with backwardness or archaism: one cannot fight against the system by waving about embellished images of a completely hypothetical past but, instead, by making massive technological investments in everyday life and finally leaving behind all purely speculative philosophy and notions of a fictitious humanity. Man's important aspect is embodied by his work, by what he strives for. Man is only genuinely human when 'striving for things' and thus participating in the process of becoming. The 'non-striving' are those who shun technology (the only lever available to us), refusing to stamp everyday life with the seal of technology and seeking to escape into the archaic and primitive, into the marginal (Marcuse!) or into neuroses (psychoanalysis!). The glorification of technology and a rejection of archaising nostalgia are truly the main traits of authentic neo-rightism, i.e. of Fayean neo-rightism. They stem directly from a careful reading of Henri Lefebvre's work.

In his *Differentialist Manifesto*, one finds additional parallels between the author's post-Marxism and the neo-rightism espoused by Faye, with the former having undoubtedly fertilised the latter: a criticism of the processes of homogenisation and a call for 'differential powers' (which must relinquish their defensive positions so as to take the offensive). Although 'repressive-oppressive' homogenisation is indeed dominant and seemingly victorious, it fails to put a definite end to particularistic resistances: despite everything, the latter can then impose a sort of polycentrism, one that is induced by the 'planetary struggle to differ' and is to be consolidated. If we ever put an end to this struggle and the repressive/oppressive powers were to secure a conclusive victory, this would signify the end of analysis, the failure of action, and the demise of discovery and creation.

From his reading of Lefebvre's *State in the Modern World*, Faye seems to have drawn a few other key ideas, notably that of a 'total mystification' that is concomitant with planetary homogenisation, in which the state is sometimes exalted (from Hobbes to Stalinism) and sometimes underestimated (from Descartes to illusions of 'pure knowledge') and where genders, the individual, the elite, structure (that of stagnant structuralists) and superabundant information serve, in turn, to mystify the public. Next comes the idea that the state should not be seen as some sort of 'mortal completion' or an 'end', but rather as a 'theatre of struggle and a battlefield'. Although the state itself will indeed come to an end, this will not mark the actual cessation (of the political). Last but not least, what Faye retained from this book was Lefebvre's call for what is 'differential', meaning for 'that which eludes repetitive identity', 'that which never reproduces, but produces', and 'that which struggles against entropy and the space of death in order to conquer a differential collective identity'.

Faye's reading of Henri Lefebvre and his meetings with the latter are interesting for more than one reason: we can now retrospectively say that a certain chemistry undoubtedly existed between the two men, certainly because Lefebvre was a former surrealist and thus able to comprehend the unstable, bubbling and turbulent mixture that Faye embodied; a mixture, in fact, of critical anarchism directed against routine-based states and of recourse to (charismatic) political authority, which shall shatter, through the very power of its decisions, a routine that remains unable to face up to the unforeseen, to wars or to disasters. If we describe Faye's approach as 'aestheticising' (which is certainly a leap), his aesthetics can only be the 'aesthetics of terror' defined by Karl Heinz Bohrer, in which a fusion of intuitionism (the Bergsonian kind with Faye) and (Schmittian) decision-making reveals suddenness and unforeseen or impromptu events — i.e. that which Faye termed an *Ernstfall*, in accordance with a certain Schmittian school — as a manifestation that is both vital and catastrophic, with life and history being an uninterrupted stream of disasters that excludes any and all tranquillity. The permanent struggle that Lefebvre called for, the perpetual cry for what is 'differential' (so that neither men nor things remain stagnant and 'Eleatic'), the very real but brief time of suddenness, the *Kairos*, the unexpected or the unusual postulated by the surrealists and their epigones, and the shock resulting from the state of emergency, which Schmitt and Freund considered essential, are all concepts or visions that converge in this Fayean synthesis. They render it inseparable from the bodies of doctrine that were debated in Paris during the 1960s and 1970s and prevent us from concluding that there actually could be some kind of consubstantiality with the phantasmagorical 'fascism' or 'extreme-rightism' that has been lent to *his* New Right ever since the moment when, frightened by the numerous instances of philosophical boldness on the 'left', 'right' and 'elsewhere and everywhere', the system began to demand that a backward step be taken and a reduction to minimal moralism take place — an infamous task that has been tackled by Bernard-Henry Lévy, Guy Konopnicki, Luc Ferry and Alain Renaut, thus paving the way for the platitudes of our *political correctness.*

All that is left for us to do is to attempt to explain Faye's Nietzscheanism and re-situate it, if at all possible, in the context of the French Nietzscheanism that lasted from the 1960s to the 1980s; but what is it that distinguishes his implicit (and sometimes explicit) Nietzscheanism from the one professed elsewhere, whether in French universities, among independent (and even marginal) philosophers or among other protagonists of the New Right?

1) If the Nietzscheanism taught at university level is complex, too complex to be used by metapolitical associations such as G.R.E.C.E.;

2) if the arabesques, meanders, rhizomes,[16] arrangements, transversals,[17] multilinearities and ritornellos[18] of an original and

---

16   TN: In philosophy, the term 'rhizome' stems from the thoughts and writings of Gilles Deleuze and Felix Guattari. The two argued that the 'arborescence' of Western logic and philosophy, in which a small idea (a seed or acorn) takes root and vertically grows into a tree of knowledge and practice, may have applied in the context of the modern Western world, but is no longer prevalent in the post-modern one. Indeed, post-modern culture bears a greater resemblance to a rhizome, a somewhat elongated usually horizontal subterranean plant stem, since, according to the two authors, it has no centre, no point of origin, and no specific shape, unity or structure. It thus grows from everywhere and is the same at all points, and because of its lack of centre (or seed), can only be uprooted or destroyed with great difficulty.

17   TN: It would seem that 'transversals' are to be understood as new directions in philosophy.

18   TN: Recurring passages.

fertile Nietzschean philosopher such as Gilles Deleuze, for instance, revealed a vocabulary that was as original as it was surprising, but remained largely misunderstood outside the faculties of philosophy at the time of the New Right's heyday (they would only have encountered misunderstanding among non-philosophers, even at university; in Italy, Francesco Ingravalle had the merit of drawing up an excellent synopsis of Nietzschean approaches, by bringing Deleuze's contribution to light in a clear fashion; see F. Ingravalle, *Nietzsche illuminista o illuminato? Guida alla lettura di Nietzsche attraverso Nietzsche*, Ed. di Ar, Padova, 1981);

3) if the more marginalised, less academic and solitary philosophers worked thoroughly on Nietzschean themes that were more circumstantial and clearly less politicisable or metapolitisable;

4) if the (sometimes scattered, sometimes concentrated) fragments of an extreme rightist heritage, spontaneously transposed into the clumsy metapolitics of the most modest grassroots activists involved in the early stages of G.R.E.C.E., conceived a very hieratic, frigid and stagnant Nietzscheanism, naively embracing a literal interpretation of the discourse on the 'Superman' and especially the latter's travesties at the hands of the Anglo-Saxon cinematographic propaganda during the two world wars, a propaganda that blended together clichés such as the 'Hun', the 'blonde beast', the caricatural madness of genetics professors wearing a nervous grin and large pair of glasses and, last but not least, the arrogance and disdain attributed to the officers of the *Freikorps* or stormtroopers;

5) if the 'super-humanism' advocated by Giorgio Locchi, understood as the type of Nietzscheanism that enjoys strong support in the speeches of G.R.E.C.E. members, insisted on overcoming the philosophical and scientific avatars of the passive and levelling type of egalitarianism resulting from Christianity and transformed into 'science' in the wake of positivism and Marxism;

6) if Pierre Chassard's theories on Nietzsche's anti-providentialism, which were incorporated by G.R.E.C.E. in the early 1970s as a result of a lack of original interpretations regarding the philosopher of Sils-Maria, insisted on the ultimate impossibility to create a completed, closed world that would no longer be characterised by any vicissitudes, tragic events, turmoil or conflictuality,

Faye's own Nietzscheanism would inscribe itself into this space, a space whose outlines are blurry and lies somewhere between the sphere of laughter and that of the tragic, as highlighted by Alexis Philonenko in his approach to Nietzsche's work (see A. Philonenko, *Nietzsche. Le Rire et le Tragique*,[19] LGF, 1995).

Indeed, the world's very fabric is fundamentally tragic in Faye's eyes, and will remain so in spite of the wishful thinking formulated by Christians, post-Christians, the proponents of natural law, etc. Following in the footsteps of Jules Monnerot, whose thoughts were systematically centred around 'heterotelia' (i.e. the fact that one always attains a different objective from that which one had assigned oneself in one's dreams and plans), Faye constantly writes about and affirms the notion according to which the political efforts, institutional constructions and obstacles clumsily put in place by censors that long to avoid a re-dealing of the cards will always end up being swept away; but before such well-deserved disappearance and necessary cleansing can come to pass, the agitations, tantrums, objurgations and admonitions stemming from those who want the same rules to forever remain in force, for centuries on end, must arouse the laughter of all impertinent realists who accept and affirm the world's tragicality and the finitude of all things. In this sense, 'laughter is a naked and truly multifaceted kind of power' to Faye, as stated by Philonenko, who adds that, in *Thus Spoke Zarathustra*, laughter is also 'the key that opens all locks', precisely because it enables one to jump over obstacles which, in fact, are no obstacles at all and to look through the cracks

---

19   TN: Laughter and the Tragic.

or beyond the seemingly monolithic masses. Nietzsche's conception of laughter is not one of substance, but of a *meta-critical function* that not only makes life itself possible (while freeing it from both gravity and anachronisms), but, as added by Philonenko, also enables 'authentic existence', in the sense that 'authenticity' is, in such a context, synonymous with fullness and innovative brilliance — unlike stagnant routines (and, in Faye's eyes, stagnant traditions), which remain 'inauthentic' and devoid of interest. One can thus say that the fascination exerted upon Faye by Heidegger's post-Nietzschean reflections on the sad 'reign of the One'[20] (and by the French writers who, each in their own way, praised the 'royal roads') had hardly any impact on the thoughts of the New Right's only true original thinker.

Nietzsche and, unconsciously, Faye himself thereafter imagined laughter which, 'having brought down the pillars of civilisation' (of the rigid and disillusioned civilisation that was both bequeathed to us and imposed upon us by the *Aufklärung* through an ever-increasing range of police methods), would channel the superman into being, meaning our overcoming of the 'human, all too human' condition, one that keeps us imprisoned in cages of legality that have lost all legitimacy, in the golden cells of a civilisation of material abundance and spiritual deficiencies. It is in this critique of civilisation, no longer driven by the idyllic and neo-pastoralist eros of 'Marcuso-Rousseauism' but, instead, by laughter and mischievousness, that we must draw a parallel with the German Conservative Revolution, which rejects this 'civilisation' either in the name of the simultaneously traumatic and exhilarating

---

20 TN: In the original German version of *Being and Time*, Heidegger uses the term *das Man*, of which there is no exact English rendition. It has been translated in several different ways, including 'the They', 'People' and 'Anyone', but the most logical and grammatically accurate English translation is 'one' ('the One', according to some versions). As for me, I would opt for the removal of the definite article to suit the English language, since Heidegger's actual use of 'das Man' was intended to explain inauthentic modes of existence as part of which a person's *Dasein* does not choose to do something, but does so merely because 'that is what *one* does' (and not 'the One does').

experience undergone by World War I soldiers or in the name of an Oriental, Asian or Russian-Orthodox faith that has apparently been modernised under the tinsel of Bolshevism. Nietzschean/Fayean super-humanity is therefore not a dauntless humanity of gendarmes characterised by their zygomatic, muscular and hieratic stiffness (with the sole, notable exception of some parts of Faye's comic strip, which is fraught with contentious topics and entitled *Avant-guerre*[21]); nor is it, as dictated by the spatiotemporal context, an anachronistic duplicate of the 'soldier nationalism' advocated by the Jünger brothers or Schauwecker, nor even a traditionalist sort of fideism tinged with orientalism. What it is, instead, is a super-humanity borne by a band of joyous, creative and impertinent scamps that evade all norms and standards. The bearers of 'civilisation', who have either forgotten how to laugh or have stifled laughter within themselves, erect paper idols, moral codes and entirely mental conventions, which, in fact, obliterate and repress the *Lebenswelt*, this instantaneous obviousness that only laughter is capable of grasping, capturing, and 'completely unlocking'. This commitment to saving the *Lebenswelt* is the leitmotif, which allows one to understand Faye's simultaneous infatuation with Heidegger, Habermas, Monnerot, Freund, Schmitt, Jünger (in his *Worker*) and Simmel, as well as his personal synthesis of all these philosophers, political scientists and sociologists, who seem very different from one another. Later on, Michel Maffesoli would undoubtedly become the academic who devised a very similar corpus to Faye's own vision (i.e. a brilliant, Dionysian and sparling one), but at a philosophical and sociological level that enjoys full university recognition, whether in France itself or internationally. This is what had to be said, or so it seems to me, about Faye's Dionysian Nietzscheanism, one that marked the New Right so very deeply. Had he polished and re-polished his intuitions in accordance with the criteria of an academic approach, Faye would indeed have been the thinker who could have become a

---

21   TN: Prelude to War.

philosopher standing halfway between Freund and Maffesoli, meaning one who would take into account the essential imperatives of the political without absolutising them, always leaving the doors wide open to allow the manifestations of Life (i.e. the *Lebenswelt*) to seep in. If Freund, ever faithful to Carl Schmitt in this regard, did not waste much time dwelling on all the bustling, outbursts and infatuations that could give rise to a thousand and one pretexts for 'occasionalism', Maffesoli does sometimes go too far, it would seem, when overestimating suburban phenomena (such as tribes) and simultaneously announcing the end of the political within the Dionysian. Faye, who had left the serious sphere of politics behind, could have bridged the gap that separated Freund from Maffesoli (with the latter having been the pupil of the Alsatian political scientist) insofar as, to him, politics should only come into play in case of an *Ernstfall* (of a dangerous, exceptional situation), disappearing as soon as the danger itself vanishes. In this respect, 'politics flows back and forth between *imperium* and anarchy', as Christiane Pigacé, who was also Julien Freund's disciple, pointed out during the First FACE²² conference in July 1993.

This Nietzscheanism, which lay halfway between laughter and tragedy and amounted to a bet on both 'naked power' and the 'meta-critical function', also found it difficult to make itself understood — not among the young activists of G.R.E.C.E., who were all fascinated by this kind of ardour, but within the movement's 'holy of holies', i.e. at its very peak, where no sun shone and no warmth reigned, and where a cantankerous mood constantly spewed out miasmas that were as unhealthy as they were undefinable; all this in an atmosphere full of foul swirls of nicotine, in which an ever-confused face and a pout that constantly belched out gratuitous insults revealed, to all lucid individuals blessed with the ability to see things clearly, what was fundamentally a parody, one that Nietzsche would have ridiculed most generously. In no way did the petty vanities of a certain

---

22   TN: *Fédération des Activités Communautaires en Europe* (The Federation of European Community Activities).

guru tolerate the development of some sort of 'meta-criticism' centred around 'liberating laughter', which always begins with a healthy capacity for self-mockery. As for Faye, he never hesitated to get himself noticed, to laugh at his own images, fantasies, tastes and sentences, which he took to absurd extremes so as to ensure that they never sunk into the quagmire of intellectual dead ends, etc. In order to question yourself, you must, in fact, be able to take each idea you develop to the point of absurdity, to realise at all times the derisory nature of your own vanities and fantasies and be aware of the ridiculousness of those petty camouflage attempts that we practice in the futile hope of impressing the gallery someday and having an 'irreproachable image' in the eyes of the media, which are controlled by the 'system that kills peoples' — a fact which ultimately indicates that one could not care less about one's own people, regardless of all the speeches one gives in one's desire to impress the public. One has always failed at exercising such self-mockery at the highest levels of G.R.E.C.E., which obviously claimed that it was not actually G.R.E.C.E. but rather a simple and fortuitous core site that had no connection to some vague 'personal strategy' of entryism in the media or to a desire to participate in the debates (?) of the *Tout-Paris*.[23]

This is why the machine, set up by a compiler aligning citations and references in the sole hope of showing off, ended up running idle 'at some point'. In the end, this 'Nietzscheanism of laughter' remains the basis of Faye's post-G.R.E.C.E.-ist efforts, from the launch of *J'ai tout compris*[24] (1987–1988), which merged grating irony with caustic satire, political messages and trendy style, to *Skyrock* radio programmes (with their *huuuuge* pranks) or even the hilarious inquiries conducted in *Écho des Savannes* and *Paris Match*, where one witnessed Faye in the

---

23 TN: The '*Tout-Paris*' (French for '*All-of-Paris*') is an expression that refers to the city's fashionable and affluent elites, whose members attend trendy events, frequent popular places and set new trends in upper-class culture.

24 A magazine whose title can be translated as 'I got it all' or 'I understand everything'.

role of 'Professor Kervous', a friend of Bill Clinton's (who had just been elected to the White House). Kervous himself looked like a typical proponent of the 1968 events and was flanked by his sprightly British secretary, 'Mary Patch' (!). He would approach some French politicians and ask them, on behalf of 'Mr President Bill Clinton', if they were prepared to apply for the post of "Secretary of State for European Affairs' in the new American 'administration'... Such practices of the Fayean New Right's 'meta-critical/metapolitical theory' are, however, a different matter, which has no place in this introduction.

II

But how was Guillaume Faye, whose charisma was undeniable, driven out of the group to which he gave a real backbone? Emblematic, his expulsion proves that the internal logic of G.R.E.C.E. has been, and remains, one of ejection. Throughout its history, the movement has excluded more officials than it has actually recruited! Some paranoid minds have deduced that this strategy of successive expulsions has been abided by in the implementation of 'given orders', orders whose purpose is to prevent France from developing an ideology that is extremely critical of the republican, Enlightenment-based, legal and administrative anachronisms that have been leading this country towards intellectual drying-up and institutional petrification, so that no sufficiently well-informed current of opinion would ever demand extensive reforms or lay down the requirements for a second French Revolution that would sweep away the institutionalised revolutionary bourgeoisie, its Enlightenment-inspired clubs and its omnipotent civil servants, including the prefects that govern a total of 95 French departments without having been elected, in flagrant contradiction with the democratic principles of the European Union! The theory of 'acting under command' has been proposed by Mexican professor Santiago Ballesteros Walsh, although I myself cannot endorse his demonstrative approach... Indeed, there is nothing to directly support

Ballesteros Walsh's hypothesis, a fact that should not, however, prevent us from noting that in nearly thirty years of existence, the Parisian New Right has failed to propose one single coherent reform of our French institutions and to contribute to the deepening of a 'regionalism' or 'subsidiarity' that could have served as a lever for a general questioning of the Jacobin system, which was directly inspired by the Enlightenment. Nor has it been able to suggest any economic reform project based on Gaullist 'participationism', the theories of François Perroux or any non-conformist economic thoughts. These failings and the persistent refusal to tackle such subjects are, at the very least, bizarre, perhaps even highly suspicious. Faye never stopped calling for the inclusion of such steps in the New Right's corpus. Was this the real reason behind his own ejection and that of all others who were also driven out? In discussions held by G.R.E.C.E. leaders, two other bizarre strategies are often mentioned: a marking strategy and one of denigration. The marking strategy is alleged to involve luring intellectuals into riding on the New Right's coattails so that they are forever marked by this and thus prevented from pursuing their research. The denigration strategy, on the other hand, consists in pitting militants against each other, labelling them 'idiots' or 'madmen' as part of a preventive measure whose purpose is to inhibit any autonomous collaboration between them beyond the headquarters' control. One would thus, for example, approach a certain independent publisher and say that 'Steuckers (or Faye, Battarra, etc.) is a dangerous, raving lunatic, perhaps even a Nazi-Trotskyist or a national-revolutionary activist, a worthy heir to the Russian *Narodnaya Volia*[25] (Steucker's own magazine is, in fact, entitled *Vouloir*,[26] isn't it?)', so that he would

---

25   TN: In the 19th century, *Narodnaya Volya* was a Russian revolutionary political organisation that sought to assassinate government officials in an effort to topple the autocratic system and impede the reforms desired by Alexander II.

26   TN: *Vouloir* was a multidisciplinary cultural magazine initially connected with a vast array of so-called 'new-rightist' publications before separating itself from

reject any manuscripts sent by that sub-Nechayev[27] of a Steuckers; with Steuckers himself being told twenty minutes later by the very same person that this publisher is 'a pleasant but foolish man caught up in the quirkiest *Völkisch* ruralist sects', to ensure that one does not entrust him with any manuscripts...

At the request of some well-known expelled individuals and some former G.R.E.C.E. executives, all of whom have been wallowing in bitterness since the failure of their constructive reformism within the movement (in which they themselves were once involved as activists), it seems useful to me to paint a summarising and comprehensive picture of this unbroken sequence of expulsions, placing particular emphasis on Faye's case.

Having been part of—and active in—circles very close to the 'centre' (despite his unawareness of who the organisation's real sponsors were, for none of its members, or even its leaders, knew them), Faye was not sufficiently wary of the fragility of his own position: indeed, he was both naive and trusting. He remained foreign to this environment and outside it, for that is where he had come from. Those who claimed to be 'initiates' never allowed him to integrate and he was always considered a 'tough nut to crack'. The most obvious indication of Faye's non-belonging to the 'core nucleus' were the poor wages he received. I still cannot comprehend how he could ever have been weak enough to be content with such a situation and to have made two mistakes:

- that of having had excessive confidence in his own charisma and having often worked too quickly, through flashes of brilliance

---

the latter in 1992. It was founded in November 1983 by Robert Steuckers and Jean-Eugène van der Taelen.

27 TN: Sergey Gennadiyevich Nechayev (2nd October, 1847–21st November/3rd December, 1882) was a Russian communist revolutionary often linked with the nihilist movement and famous for his unquenchable thirst for revolution, using any means necessary, including terrorism and revolutionary terror.

and independently, failing, at times, to support his texts with adequate references and to give them proper weight. The ideal situation would have involved Faye being supported by a team that would have explored the library universe for him, passed on bibliographies and book summaries to him, attended academic and political conferences on his behalf, etc. Unfortunately, Faye did not surround himself with people capable of doing such work for him. In the medium term, this would constitute a great loss.

- Secondly, Faye lacked a personal and autonomous tool that would have provided him with a way out and enabled him to resume his activity independently, by redirecting the audience he had recruited within G.R.E.C.E. towards his own person (his own circle or magazine, for instance). Faye never organised the network of his own connections, nor did he maintain structured relationships with the personalities that he was required to meet with on his numerous journeys. Once ejected, he found himself all alone, without a portfolio, platform or his own resources. Because of the very movement which he himself had endowed with so much vigour, his intellectual quest had to come to an end. The basic principles of political activity teach us that it is necessary, under all circumstances, to keep one's exit door handy, so as to fall back on one's own feet in the event of expulsion and re-initiate the dynamics autonomously — even against one's former partners, if necessary.

These few reflections on Faye's person force us to retrace the chronology of his 'G.R.E.C.E.-ist' itinerary. As Taguieff writes (op. Cit.), this journey began within the framework of the Vilfredo Pareto Circle, dominated by the personality of Yvan Blot (alias Michel Norey), today a *Front National* MEP. Faye, who worked in the automobile industry at the time, mastered his oratorical techniques there under the instigation of a former militant of the French radical Right who had relinquished all militancy. Unquestionably, Faye was a good student, which I quickly noticed in 1976 upon meeting him for the first time in Brussels, in the hall of the Ramada Hotel at *Chaussée de Charleroi*, where he delivered a fiery speech on 'Europe, the U.S. colony'. Following in the footsteps of Giorgio Locchi, who had put together an entire *Nouvelle école* issue to stigmatise the American hold on Europe and highlight the radical differences between the European mind and the American one, Faye immediately shifted gears to embrace the anti-Americanism strongly supported by the Italian philosopher and definitively broke with all the 'Westernist' temptations of the French Right, including those of certain survivors of *Europe Action*, an activist movement of the 1960s in which a large number of G.R.E.C.E. executives had initially made their debut.

In 1977–1978, the first wave of division struck the New Right, which was still little known to the general public. On the one hand, Yvan Blot, Jean-Yves Le Gallou and a few others founded the '*Club de l'Horloge*',[28] whose strategy was to invade the political sphere, the professional domain (mainly the managerial one) and the most prestigious schools of Paris (the ENA,[29] etc.) at a time when Alain de Benoist was betting on a 'fight for ideas', both in the press and the general media. The *Club de l'Horloge* opted for liberal or national-liberal endeavours. Although Alain de Benoist had the merit of keeping clear of this march towards 'respectability' (which did, however, announce the return of liberalism in the debates of the 80s), he did not outline any coherent and structured alternative to Giscardism and the elements of social democracy that pervaded French society following de Gaulle's disappearance. Faye rejected liberal logic, all in the name of the discourse which he defended in the columns of *Cahiers du Cercle Vilfredo Pareto*. He felt that his statist, autarkist and 'regal' ideas could not be defended on the rostrum of the *Club de l'Horloge* and thus remained with de Benoist in G.R.E.C.E… His motivations

---

28 TN: Clock Club.

29 TN: The *École nationale d'administration*, or National School of Administration.

were therefore purely ideological and his choice dictated neither by material interests nor professional opportunities.

Philippe Marceau then entered the scene in G.R.E.C.E. and structured the latter with formidable efficacy. Thanks to his dedication and generosity, Faye found a solid framework, one that was worthy of him. Marceau disciplined the spirited horse that Faye undoubtedly was and ensured that he was properly paid. Faye would give things his best from 1978 to 1982, a period during which he would benefit from the organisational rigour imposed by Philippe Marceau. In addition, G.R.E.C.E. managed to score some points at the time, founding its Copernic editions in 1978 (though the latter would go bankrupt in 1981) and flooding the editorial staff in Louis Pauwels' *Figaro-Magazine*. Faye was smitten, as were many others, including myself. He believed that the future lay in 'meta-politics'. At that stage of the movement's history, so did Marceau.

At the end of 1981, in spite of the officially anti-American and anti-liberal discourse, Alain de Benoist developed a 'personal strategy', undoubtedly seeking to outpace the *Club de l'Horloge*. Such would be the 'liberal alternative' adventure, an ambitious project to organise a gigantic conference in Paris, with the support of *Figaro Magazine*. This conference was intended to bring together all the French theorists of political and economic liberalism, including Raymond Aron, as well as their American counterparts and mentors, including the Chicago Boys, etc. It was, however, Alain de Benoist *himself* who would force his way into the very centre of this 'Areopagus'.[30] Alerted by some good journalistic consciences, several prospective participants refused to speak if the 'Nazi' (?) de Benoist stepped onto the rostrum. The incurred costs were such that the organisers and sponsors could no longer back down, and Alain de Benoist was simply ousted. The conference did take place, with *Figaro-Magazine* echoing it all. 'Liberal alternative', however, ceased to exist the day after the event. This little

---

30 TN: The supreme tribunal of Athens.

adventure speaks volumes about the lack of sincerity characterising the New Right's leader: in order to achieve stardom, he was willing to sell his anti-liberalism and anti-Americanism cheaply and discard his Europeanism/neo-Gaullist positions, Germanophilia and cult of the 'Conservative Revolution'. I remember seeing a very sceptical and highly doubtful Faye at the time, a Faye who was an honest man and had always followed his own ideas rather than chase political or media opportunities... He seemed distraught; distraught to find that others were willing to make statements that contradicted all that they had always said, all in a desire to hold a minor position, take advantage of an opportunity or follow a (Parisian) trend.

In January 1982, an issue of *Éléments* magazine[31] entitled '*Mourir pour Gdansk?*'[32] is published. In it, Alain de Benoist rejects all pro-Western logic (although he had been ready to sacrifice many things to it no more than a month earlier!) and argues against the NATO maximalists, who had expressed their concern about Jaruselski's assumption of power in Poland; he dismantles the myth of the Soviet enemy and declares that the Soviet system — which he does not, however, endorse — is actually less dangerous for European culture than American fashions and films and wages what is, in fact, a pre-emptive war against Reaganism, which had just taken over the White House. This well-constructed and courageous sort of anti-Westernism angers Raymond Bourgine, the head of *Valeurs actuelles*[33] and *Spectacle du Monde*,[34] a weekly and monthly magazine in which Alain de Benoist had begun and from which most sections of *Vu de droite*[35] actually stem. Alain de Benoist is expelled from the editorial staff. Although this marks G.R.E.C.E.'s first major failure, Alain de Benoist keeps his

---

31   TN: With Alain de Benoist acting as its editor, *Éléments* is a French bimonthly magazine that has been published since 1973.

32   TN: To Die for Gdansk?

33   TN: *Current Values.*

34   TN: Literally *The Spectacle of the World.*

35   TN: *View from the Right*, published by Arktos Media Ltd. in 3 volumes.

'idea column' in *Le Figaro Magazine* (which he would be deprived of a few months later).

Soon, Philippe Marceau apprehended that the situation was deteriorating. Being a good businessman, he felt that his investments in G.R.E.C.E. had not borne the expected fruit; his financial effort had been too great for the meagre results obtained. He probably believed that the successive failures which the movement had just suffered (the bankruptcy of Copernic editions, the failure of 'liberal alternative', the ousting from Bourgine's publications, G.R.E.C.E.'s faltering position in *Le Figaro Magazine*, the decreasing media attention, the relentlessness of opponents, etc.) did not bode well. Marceau realised that he had failed to overcome the movement's 'flaws' (the presence of 'decision makers behind the scenes', the mismanagement of funds, the whims and personal strategies, the inability to abide by a specific line, ideological variations in accordance with current trends, etc.). He found that the books which some had assured him would be written had not been written at all, that the budgeted funds had to be used to plug further gaps, etc. He thus came to the conclusion that 'meta-politics' had failed. Using G.R.E.C.E.'s networks and files, he attempted to set up regional *forums*, whose intended role was to organise the opposition against Mitterrand[36] and the socialists who had just seized power during the elections of May and June 1981. In order to oppose the socialists and the supporters of the 1968 events, who had gained access to the command posts of French society, a network of political clubs became a necessity — and that is where Marceau thought the future lay. The political cards he played in right-wing Gaullist circles, however, amounted to nothing. Compelled to dissolve the regional forums, Marceau left the stage. G.R.E.C.E. was thus deprived of the advantage of having a formidable organiser and a patron who never counted his gifts. Marceau's exit marked the end of both rigour and the apparatus'

---

36   TN: François Maurice Adrien Marie Mitterrand (26th October, 1916–8th January, 1996) was a French statesman and the longest serving President of France (having remained in power from 1981 to 1995).

disciplined organisation. Two years later, Marceau would find himself in Le Pen's party, where his generosity and appreciation of the importance of work would allow him to give the best of himself.

With the departure of this exceptional, honest and scrupulous man, Faye was destabilised, losing all protection and guarantees. He had not followed Marceau; being anti-liberal and hardly drawn to conservative political circles on the fringes of the RPR or within it, Faye still believed in 'meta-politics'. One proceeded to deceive him and lured him in with promises of a return to the 1978 situation (the founding of a new publishing house, the creation of a new weekly, etc.). While alone with a few friends in early 1983, Faye hosted three brilliant days of his CRMC (*Collectif de Réflexion sur le Monde Contemporain*[37]) in the space of eight months. After these three days of exceptional intellectual quality, however, the CRMC disappeared, Faye having failed to maintain this circle, one which could have granted him full autonomy. From 1982 to 1985, he participated in the 'Athens Colloquiums', organised by the rector of the University of the Greek capital, Jason Hadjidinas, who, having encouraged Faye to resume his studies and write a doctorate thesis, passed away prematurely. Faye then taught 'sociology of sexuality' courses at the University of Besançon. In 1985, while at the University of Mons, he took the floor at a major Euro-Arab conference, where he undoubtedly set the tone, his oratorical talents impressing the Vatican's representative, Father Michel Lelong, during the entire initiative (which had been launched by Professor Safar)! The day after the conference, a few dozen G.R.E.C.E. executives gathered so as to attempt a revival in the shape of the *Institut Européen des Arts et des Lettres*[38] (IEAL), which, unfortunately, would remain short-lived. After the passing of Jason Hadjidinas, who had encouraged Faye in a paternal manner and strived to cure his heartbreaking naiveté (but to no avail), Faye found himself increasingly

---

37   TN: Collective of Reflections on the Contemporary World.

38   TN: European Institute of Arts and Letters.

isolated. He no longer participated in major conferences, neither in France nor elsewhere. Under the pseudonym Gérald Fouchet, he wrote some excellent articles and exceptional interviews in *Magazine Hebdo*, a news service run by Alain Lefèvre. Smothered by publicists ever hostile to the New Right, however, *Magazine Hebdo* was forced to cease its publications. Faye was thus left with no other income but his very meagre permanent-member salary in G.R.E.C.E. The years of 1986 and 1987 brought nothing but stagnation to him. Treacherously orchestrated propaganda described him all over Europe as a 'fanatic', a 'madman' and a 'drug addict', words which, to my great amazement, I myself heard when at Armin Mohler's back in July 1984. 'One' had spread the fictional story of a slightly insane and simple-minded Faye, and especially that of a muddleheaded Faye, whose articles 'one' had to rewrite...

Shortly before the Mons conference and the death of Rector Hadjidinas, Jean-Claude Cariou, the (then) Secretary General of G.R.E.C.E. and a lad whose exceptional devotion bordered on holiness, attempted to salvage things. Being the one who organised, from his office in Paris, the movement's conference and colloquium programmes and its other initiatives in the provinces, he knew all too well that, without Faye, G.R.E.C.E. would be doomed to dry up. Faye himself was, however, paralysed by his insignificant salary, which, since the departure of the generous Marceau, he perceived as mere alms, as if it were a bone thrown to a stray dog. Cariou thus suggested reforming the movement, a process that was to involve:

- giving Faye a decent salary, a proposal rejected by the new patrons, two fellows who, although only half-literate, still displayed immeasurable pretentiousness. Cariou's first suggestion shows how dependent and 'financially assisted' Faye actually was (a situation that led to his being repeatedly targeted with reproach). There is a lesson to be learned here by all young aspirants to 'metapolitical struggle'.

- a general amendment of salaries and the supervising of accounts by a regularly elected board;

- a definitive rejection of 'occult power', i.e. espousing transparency;

- and the movement's rejuvenation.

A few days after formulating these reasonable proposals, Cariou found himself excluded following the staging of a grotesque scene during which he was made to appear before a sort of hastily assembled tribunal, one that was comprised of completely illiterate lackeys that shouted slogans, which they had learned by heart and who, of course, knew nothing of all the intricacies of 'metapolitical struggle' nor of the ideas that their movement was supposed to defend. And this is where the entire parodic dimension of the New Right's Parisian adventure came to light. The preposterous idea of organising such a tribunal shows that the philosophical claims made by this group of immature individuals were nothing more than deception. The written testimony left by Cariou inthe shape of a letter is quite eloquent in this regard: while these operetta-worthy Fouquier-Tinvilles[39] vociferated and spewed out their hostilities, a pallid Alain de Benoist floundered in his adjacent office, alone and in a state of pitiful hyper-nervousness, awaiting the end of this vaudeville[40] performance. It was only after the latter had finished that the pontiff himself came out of his lair and stammered to the victim: *do not destroy my movement*,[41] repeating

---

39   TN: Antoine Quentin Fouquier de Tinville was a prosecutor during the French Revolution and its Reign of Terror. Hence the comparison and the allusion to a G.R.E.C.E.-related reign of terror.

40   TN: Originally, a vaudeville was a light and comic theatrical performance devoid of psychological or moral intentions and meant to entertain. Used in this context, it is to be understood as a pathetic masquerade.

41   TN: De Benoist used a French slang expression, *'faire un* destroy', which, when translated literally into English, results in a non-sensical phrase, namely 'make a destroy'. The French expression itself refers to the punk rock practice of destroying everything and has no real equivalent in the English language.

this injunction three or four times in a row, mechanically and pathetically, his stomach in knots and with a tone of remorse that would only be fleeting, just as his remorse always is. Cariou's mistake lay, first of all, in not having laughed out loud at these puppets and bowed out, punctuating his departure with Homeric snickering and leaving those miserable acrobatic entertainers hanging, without further ado, so that they may glimpse, were it only for a brief moment, their own finitude, their own dereliction; and, secondly, in not having detailed his misadventure in a brochure, one that we would have gladly distributed. This negligence allowed the illiterate to control the movement and to make and break its executive body in accordance with their cramped brains' own whims. What a sad involution that was!

With Cariou now gone, Gilbert Sincyr would attempt to put the house in order, but since Faye had begun to kick over the traces and Alain de Benoist had imposed the presence of the neo-Nazi Olivier Mathieu in the '*Études et Recherches*' Circle,[42] which was Faye's only prerogative within G.R.E.C.E., Gilbert Sincyr left most hurriedly, as disgusted as the others had been before him. The 1986 party conference was a complete fiasco, turning into a farce under the leadership of the indescribably outrageous Mathieu, Alain de Benoist's favourite at the time. The conference held in November 1986 only brought together a handful of people. Marco Tarchi (the head of the Italian New Right) and I were called to the rescue in order to enrich the conference, during which Faye would deliver a speech that revealed his disappointments and resentments. And here's an anecdote: one of the illiterate individuals mobilised a few months earlier to get rid of the unfortunate Cariou — who would suffer terribly as a result of his ejection — had my wife's bag searched, suspecting her of bringing in some sort of infernal device that would blow up during the conference... Despite being so solicitous to maintain his own respectability, Alain de Benoist was, at that time, prone to choosing very peculiar

---

42 TN: Meaning 'Studies and Research' Circle.

collaborators. This anecdote betrays, in a most exemplary manner, the atmosphere of para-military childishness, tyrannical authoritarianism and Nazi hysteria that prevailed in this environment, an environment that claimed to be strictly intellectual.

In 1987, Faye proceeded to burn, once and for all, all the bridges that still tied him to G.R.E.C.E. In May of that same year, he drafted a proclamation in which he calmly took stock of his own commitment. The text was imbued with great wisdom, in contradiction with all the gossip spread about Faye, describing him as 'insane', 'alcoholic' and 'drugged up'. As part of the New Right, it was in Brussels that he would give his last lecture in September 1987, on the rostrum of Rogelio Pete's GRESPE, in a luxurious lounge at the prestigious *Hôtel Métropole*. The topic? 'Soft' ideology. Very calmly and extremely methodically, he described the mechanisms of what Huyghe had termed 'langue de co-ton'[43] and the soft totalitarianism that this watered-down language had paved the way for, heralding our current 'political correctness'. Pity that he arrived at the *Métropole* flanked by the scandalous Mathieu, who could not help talking about the 'black sun surrounded by a white circle on a red background', a lyric slip of the tongue, which his boss must have greatly appreciated in private before hiring him... The fact of having invited Faye led to my being targeted with several insults during a telephone conversation with a fiercely committed G.R.E.C.E. activist, as the movement had, in the meantime, been reorganised by the very same illiterates that had ejected Cariou... He had undoubt-edly been ordered to resort to intimidation, though this intimidation would have no effect whatsoever.

In 1987, it was the medievalist Pierre Vial who, in turn, left G.R.E.C.E. to become a member of the *Front National*, thus depriv-ing the magazines of the metapolitical movement of a vast historical

---

43   TN: Coined by François-Bernard Huyghe, a French political scientist and es-sayist, the term *'langue de coton'* (literally 'cotton language') refers to a 'diplo-matic' sort of language that consists in using a large number of words without actually saying anything meaningful.

dimension, which they would never regain. Following this departure, Jean Mabire's collaboration became scarce before finally disappearing, robbing the movement of texts characterised by their rare literary lucidity. Mabire would then offer his chronicles and writers' portraits to *National-Hebdo*,[44] enriching this political and polemical paper with literary 'miniatures' fraught with finesse and relevance.

And there we have it: the timeline of the most spectacular ejection in the history of the New Right. There have, however, been other forced departures, including that of Giorgio Locchi, who was himself driven out in 1979, stripping the movement of sound philosophical judgement, judgement that had hitherto shaped the New Right's conceptual backbone. Then came the failed integration of Ange Sampieru, who, in addition to being a brilliant jurist, constitutionalist and economist, was also a man of the '*grandes écoles*',[45] a 'statist' and a lucid critic of liberalism. Next, one witnessed the sustained attack against Thierry Mudry and Christiane Pigacé, preventing the New Right's general discourse from being permeated by an alternative sort of history (one that is genuinely centred on the people and the peasantry) as well as by a political philosophy directly drawn from Julien Freund's ideas. In 1990, one saw the ousting of the young Hugues Rondeau, the leader of 'Nouvelle Droite Jeunesse',[46] who had called for my return. A highly cultured man, Rondeau was inspired by Gaullism and had both very good literary taste and a sense of values and aesthetics that did not stem from the typical manias characterising Parisian rightist movements. Then, in 1992, came my turn to be driven out following the staging of a situation that I shall refrain from describing out of sheer pity. Finally, in 1993, it was Guillaume d'Erebe who was thrown out as if he were the very scum of the earth, depriving the movement of a very well-educated philosopher, a political scientist, and an expert

---

44   TN: *National-Hebdo* is considered the unofficial weekly of the *Front National*.

45   TN: In France, the '*grandes écoles*' are prestigious university-level colleges with competitive entrance examinations.

46   TN: New Right Youth.

in matters relating to Althusser, Spinoza, economic heterodoxies, Perroux and Carl Schmitt. The mess was an enormous one. The NR had withered away, without integrating anyone. It thus suffered a very slow death resulting from attrition, only surviving thanks to the brilliance of its own past (1978–1982): the excellence of the texts penned by those that were excluded, regardless of their personal differences or their intellectual standpoints (Faye, Sampieru, Locchi, Vial, Mabire, etc.); and the remnants of (Marceau's) organisation and (Cariou's) kindness, whose seeds had been sown by true activists. This allows us to say that the 'community', which G.R.E.C.E. prides itself on, only subsists among the excluded. The New Right's genuine community lies outside its surviving structure, where only its gravediggers now flounder.

An impartial observer of French political movements once told me that the New Right was typically Parisian, in the sense that *Action Française*,[47] the surrealist movement around Breton, and the French communists had also experienced long ejection sequences. It seems that there is indeed a Parisian model of pathological 'ejection-ism' that everyone imitates there, however unconsciously. The New Right is thus no exception to the rule.

Conclusion

These ejections have left a lot of bitterness in their wake — a feeling of having been deceived and double-crossed by a bunch of pathetic little wretches, of having strayed into a low-quality vaudeville performance. In its anti-Christian speeches, the New Right has mocked the Gospel's precept of turning the other cheek when the right one has just been slapped. Let us, therefore, not accept injustice in a self-righteous

---

47 TN: Advocating anti-parliamentarian, anti-Semitic and very nationalistic views, *Action Française* (French for 'French Action') was a prominent right-wing and antirepublican group active in France during the first four decades of the 20th century.

fashion,[48] in the hope of later being granted access to paradise or to a 'position' in a G.R.E.C.E. movement that one would be expected to resuscitate. They must be made to pay the price for what they have done, especially to Faye and Cariou, as well as Marceau. Those who have deliberately, for personal considerations or despicable material interests, broken the New Right's momentum, sapped Faye's energy and his flashes of brilliance, and killed his emerging affirmative Habermasism in the bud must now be made to pay the piper. We must now build, build what Faye never had the opportunity to construct, while remaining faithful, unshakably faithful to his memory, his ideas, and his commitment of old. That is precisely why we are still here, keeping up the good work and ever mindful of the saying coined by William of Orange, i.e. William the Taciturn: 'It is not necessary to hope in order to act, nor to succeed so as to persevere'.

Robert Steuckers,
October 1995

---

48   TN: In the original French text, Robert Steuckers uses the adverb 'benoîtement', rooted in the adjective 'benoît' (and pronounced just like 'Benoist'), which is no coincidence at all and a passive-aggressive pun if there ever was one. The word 'benoîtement' can be translated as 'complacently', 'gullibly', 'blithely' or even 'self-righteously', with the last option suiting the text's religious references, even if all these words were, in my view, clearly aimed at Alain de Benoist himself.

I I

Farewell, Guillaume Faye, After Forty-four Years of Common Struggle

By Robert Steuckers

I LEARNED OF the death of Guillaume Faye while at the *Gare de Lyon* railway station, shortly before noon, as I was leaving on a mission to Geneva, where a meeting sponsored by Mr Pascal Junod[1] and a symposium of 'Helvetic Resistance' under the supervision of David Rouiller were to be held. I was heading there to join Pierre Krebs and Tomislav Sunic. I couldn't help but think of a detail that suddenly crossed my mind again: I had learnt of his death at the very place where he was photographed for *Figaro Magazine* alongside Roger Lemoine, the then president of G.R.E.C.E.: Louis Pauwels' weekly presented him as the one who was going to do a *Tour de France* to sell the 'New Right', which, at the time, was in full swing.

Personally, I first saw Guillaume Faye in Lille, back in 1975, when he was giving a lecture on the dangerous energy dependence afflicting Europe. His arguments were both factual and specific and reminded me of a famous author who I had already familiarised myself with most intensively at the end of my own adolescence, namely Anton Zischka (1904–1997). I had read several of his works, which I had either found at second-hand booksellers or read in the library that belonged to my father's boss, Count Guillaume de Hemricourt de Grunne (1888–1978). With regard to my final year dissertation at the end of secondary school (in 1974), I had chosen to study one of the works penned by this prolific author on the topic of Central and Eastern Europe. It was with precision that Zischka dealt with the facts of the world and without resorting to ideological embellishments; and I have just read, after forty-five years, that Ernst Jünger himself had once praised

---

1   TN: A Swiss politician and solicitor.

Zischka's style and stated that the latter was endowed with the ability to grasp all that was essential and communicate it to his readers, i.e. that he was a great 'synoptician' (*ein grosser Synoptiker*). And so was Guillaume Faye back in the 1970s, having yet another thing in common with Zischka: he believed that practical sciences and techniques could solve the political, geopolitical and agro-alimentary issues faced by our world's different peoples, provided, of course, that we relinquish and discard any and all 'ideological nuisances'. Guillaume Faye was convinced of this, despite the fact that, in his own, everyday life, there were many electrical, mechanical or technological items that he did not know how to use, even those characterised by no more than slight sophistication. And I myself am not much more fortunate than him in these areas.

At the Ramada Hotel

A few months later, I met Faye again in a room at the Ramada Hotel at *Chaussée de Charleroi in Saint-Gilles*, along with Georges Hupin, Alain Derriks, Frédéric Beerens, Piet Tommissen, etc. Slightly tipsy, Guillaume painted a succinct summary of American imperialism and presented G.R.E.C.E.'s new line of struggle, namely that of anti-Westernism, as announced in the extensive *Nouvelle école* issue on America (mainly thanks to the views expressed by Giorgio Locchi, who Faye considered his mentor). Next in line (at a later point, in 1980) was the *Éléments* issue entitled *Pour en finir avec la civilisation occidentale*,[2] whose cover was enhanced through the displaying of a beautiful and astonishing painting by Olivier Carré, representing a decaying Statue of Liberty. The anti-Westernism of our worldview had thus been launched. My comrades and I had at last found allies in the struggle that we intended to initiate, without, however, having put any order into our intuitions yet. Faye thus tore the future 'New Right' away from all the more or less Westernist ambiguities that still seemed

---

2   TN: To Put an End to Western Civilisation.

to pervade its discourse in the early 1970s. This tone of his displeased a certain group of liberal snobs, who then came to pester us during the first Belgian G.R.E.C.E. meetings in Brussels; Faye's slight intoxication when speaking in the lounges of the Ramada scandalised them, as if they were stuck-up old bats — secularistic ones in this case — that had just heard someone utter lewd words. If only you had seen their faces!

To us, it was obvious that the 'New Right', which did not yet bear this name, was basically this: a barrier of resistance to Westernism, Atlanticism, and the policies of resignation and submission that these negative forces led to all around Europe and particularly in Belgium. We expressed this rejection because we had not digested, at the time, the affair surrounding the 'deal of the century', in which the countries of the Benelux and Scandinavia had opted for American F16s, to the detriment of Bloch-Dassault and Saab aircrafts.

This barrier of resistance was visible in Jean Thiriart's case, a man who had left the political field behind and whose offices were a stone's throw from the Ramada's hall, where Faye had given his thunderous speech. It was also noticeable in the writings and speeches of both Locchi and Faye. Thiriart and his disciple Garcet had already warned us of the pusillanimity characterising G.R.E.C.E.'s own guru, whose political ideas had the 'consistency of a dish of cooked macaroni'. The following years would confirm the fact that they had been right all along to be wary of him... It was obvious, however, that such pusillanimity did not exist in Faye and Locchi's case and that they were the ones we intended to follow and support.

The 'Studies & Research' Secretariat

We thus basically chose to follow Faye, because he was so clear in his speeches and writings, and learnt quickly enough that he had become the principal presenter of G.R.E.C.E.'s 'Studies and Research' division, a division which should, in theory, have acted as the main driving force of the entire association, whose goals were officially of a 'metapolitical' nature. During G.R.E.C.E.'s 1978 colloquium, after which Giorgio Locchi would never take the floor again, we heard Faye deliver a first speech ('Contre l'économisme'[3]). In early 1979, Faye invited me to be part of the 'Studies and Research Secretariat' (S.E.R.), even before I actually became a member of the association. I then went to Paris in June 1979 in order to attend, for the very first time, a meeting of this Secretariat, where I learned, to my great disappointment, that Giorgio Locchi had left G.R.E.C.E., as he no longer wished to collaborate with the latter, specifically because the strategy of entryism targeting the hushed and upscale clubs of pro-governmental rightist movements was premature and therefore doomed to fail. His son had come to announce this decision and the declarations he made on that day aroused in me a pervasive sort of distrust towards the association itself, because what it actually fostered within itself were people that were hostile to the Italian thinker; people who were ready to stoop to anything in order to reach an agreement with a detestable regime; and people whose presence could only be harmful, as the future would confirm. It was on this day that I met Stefano Vaj, who had come especially from Milan to attend the event.

In December 1979, G.R.E.C.E. organised its annual conference, entitling it '*Contre tous les totalitarismes*'.[4] When it was Faye's turn to speak, a bunch of henchmen burst into the *Palais des Congrès* at *Porte Maillot* and ravaged the booth area, seriously injuring Jean-Louis Pesteil, a translator and Germanist colleague that I did not yet know personally, as well as Grégory Pons, who still displayed a mocking smile while covered in blood from head to toe, and a few other participants.

Hearing the noise of the fight, Faye turned up his microphone's sound to the maximum and shouted out his text, so that we would not miss a single part of his fiery speech, while a major part of the

---

3   TN: Against Economism.

4   TN: Against All Forms of Totalitarianism.

listeners descended from the stands to give chase to the furious wild-eyed fanatics that had come to disrupt the conference. I myself went down there as well and found a completely destroyed room and, at its very centre, Alain de Benoist with a menthol cigarette in the mouth, shaking his head and muttering 'What madness! What madness!', unconcerned about the projectiles flying in all possible directions. An anonymous friend of mine tore off the metal legs of a few chairs and distributed them to the new arrivals so that they could be used in the ensuing battle. I received one, too, and ran towards the skirmish in my Sunday clothing, but did not succeed in getting there: the assailants were driven back thanks to Patrice de Plunkett, who had activated the fire hose and released thick jets of water upon the troublemakers, who then fled chaotically, pursued by our most pugnacious friends, including an Armenian comrade, Jacques Karakachian (nicknamed the 'Caucasian boar'); Gérald le Pied-Noir; Jean-Pierre Van Geyt, who recently passed away and once acted as *Nouvelle école*'s long-time correspondent in Romance Belgium; Michel R., who was originally from Namur; and a young Flemish worker, who, according to what he himself told me, was employed in a 'metal mailbox factory'.

The Themistocles Savas Promotion

On 6th June, 1980, Faye arrived at Georges Hupin's place in Uccle, flanked by Philippe Millau, in order to participate in a brief presentation of my graduation work on Jordis von Lohausen's understanding of geopolitics and to subsequently give a new anti-Westernist lecture entitled '*L'Occident ou l'Europe?*'[5] in the great hall of the 'Tour du Midi', right next to the station. His speech would be heckled in a childish and obtrusive manner by the one who would become Alain de Benoist's obsequious deputy in Flanders, one who would obviously change his opinions whenever ordered by his guru: a caricatural Westernist and Americanophile with a favourable attitude towards

---

5   TN: The West or Europe?

NATO, he would soon become—on the surface, at least—an anti-American Europeanist and NATO critic. If his pontiff had asked him to be simultaneously pro-Chinese, a pan-Africanist and a Seventh-day Adventist, he would have done so as well... On that day, Faye and Millau asked me to participate in G.R.E.C.E.'s executive school during the month of July, an event which would become known as the 'Themistocles Savas Promotion', in memory of a Greek friend who had just passed away while riding his motorbike in the mountainous region of Epirus. Jason Hadjidinas, the former dean of the University of Piraeus, who would become a great friend and a staunch supporter of Faye's, was also present: he would remain loyal to him until his death in 1986, having always hoped to free him from the precariousness and dangerous financial dependence that tied him to G.R.E.C.E.'s capricious guru, who forced him to live on a minimum wage. Jason's passing was a terrible ordeal for Faye and may account for his decision to leave G.R.E.C.E. at the end of 1986 and enter the showbiz domain through Radio Skyrock. The 1980 executive school was a decisive one for me. I travelled there from Paris alongside Faye, in Pierre Bérard's car. We had picked Guillaume up at Pierre's home, a charming little apartment where his daughter had just been born. Along the way, we visited Vaison-la-Romaine and Sénanque Abbey, where I would not return until 2017. It was with them that I discovered Provence: I saw my very first lavender fields and, for the first time ever, heard the music-like sound of cicadas and observed long, grey lizards passing over our tables. In September 1980, I became a member of G.R.E.C.E., and it was Pierre Vial who would give me my card in Brussels. I promised him then that I would remain faithfully committed to our metapolitical fight; to the death. I am thus very pleased to serve him in this manner even today, although I did, in fact, leave the association in December 1981.

From March 1981 onwards, Faye and I would be colleagues on the premises of *rue Charles Lecocq* in Paris. We would remain so until the 15th of December. Alongside Michel Dejus, he was practically my sole interlocutor during this period of nine months: I got to know him as someone who was both affable and naturally kind, despite all those Nietzschean and super-humanistic rantings (which were obviously part of our own folklore). I also discovered a Guillaume who was a tintinophile[6] and an avid Franquin[7] reader, a mania that we both shared with Grégory Pons and Pascal Junod. To Faye, the character of the fat Demesmaeker in the *Gaston Lagaffe* comic books epitomised the corrupt, psycho-rigid, vain, stupid and pharisaic world, which genuine neo-rightist anthropology was meant to mock and combat (especially through telephone pranks, the kind of tomfoolery that Faye truly excelled at). Super-humanism, a term coined by Locchi, was to bring about a (super) humanity in which there would be no Demesmaekers or, alternatively, one where such people would be scolded and driven to the very margins of society. Allow me to add something to this little comic strip panorama, something that is, of course, very obvious: Zorglub's flying machines — which one encounters in the adventures of Spirou and Fantasio — were already a stimulus to the Archeofuturistic disposition characterising Faye, who, in the deep recesses of his imagination, must have begun to conceive his famous 'squalines',[8] which would later be included in his own comic strip, *Avant-guerre*.

---

6   TN: The term 'tintinophile' is a neologism referring to one's passion for the *Adventures of Tintin* comic series, which stemmed from the imagination of Georges Rémy (a.k.a. 'Hergé').

7   TN: André Franquin (3rd January, 1924–5th January, 1997) was a prominent Belgian comics artist. His most famous creations include the characters of Gaston and Marsupilami, in addition to the *Spirou et Fantasio* comic strip between 1947 and 1969, a period which, according to many fans, embodied the series' golden years.

8   TN: Faye's 'squalines' are a sort of future rocket-plane.

Pareto and Heidegger

We were given two missions at the time — to produce a *Nouvelle école* issue on Pareto and another one on Heidegger. The two themes had, of course, been suggested by Faye himself, who insisted that the magazine had to remain serious and be read at universities without arousing sarcasm. Faye's obsession lay in having the magazine include various absurdities based on pseudo-paganism, on the kind of 'paganouilleries'[9] or 'nazisteries' that the publishing director liked to indulge in, with a carelessness that left us speechless. Faye abhorred reiterated mantras and language tics that repeated *ad infinitum*, especially when they were irrelevant to real life. In Faye's eyes, any articulable kind of paganism had to reconnect with Greek antiquity and its well-structured philosophy (which remains unsurpassable in its capacity for questioning) — Heraclitus' dynamic ardour, Plato's elitism, and the logic and the rigour displayed by Aristotle in his *Politics*.

Thanks to Professor Piet Tommissen's benevolent intervention and the assistance offered by Bernard Marchand, we were able to release a tolerable issue in June, one in which Faye also published a key article on a work that has now, unfortunately, been forgotten and which the alumni generation should, once again, seek out on its library shelves: Jules Monnerot's *L'intelligence du politique*,[10] which was published in two volumes. It is more specifically the second volume of this masterful work that should be read, as it is essentially dedicated to the topic of 'doxanalysis', i.e. the analysis of the opinions that animate any and every political sphere. Monnerot, a former French surrealist, who was also close to the poets of the *négritude* movement[11] (given his Martinican origins), would later tell me that Faye's analysis of his work

---

9   TN: Just like 'nazisteries', 'paganouilleries' is a neologism that has no official English translation. In the absence of accepted renderings, the latter term can be understood as referring to 'paganistic nonsense/hogwash'.

10 TN: (The) Intelligence of the Political.

11 TN: *Négritude* is defined as a movement of critique and literary theory that was developed during the 1930s by a majority of francophone intellectuals, authors,

was the best of all, an analysis that was to be largely ignored by French universities in the name of what was already an *ante litteram* form of 'political correctness'. At the time, Faye liked to speak of 'vagaries': the world is subject to various vagaries, he kept repeating. Comforting philosophies and ideological nuisances (Raymond Ruyer) could never change anything about it, since they could never succeed in bringing the world to a halt. Having read a text taken from a *Siemens Stiftung* conference held in Munich (and chaired by Armin Mohler), I mentioned the notion of *Ernstfall*. In Monnerot's writings, we discovered the concept of *heterotelia*, a term that designates a situation that arises despite the objectives set by the decision maker's initial (and excessively rational) political will. A person's political will can, therefore, generate states of affairs that contradict their initial project and any well-structured programme that has been shaped in harmony with sheer logic. In the conversations we had back then, we combined numerous reflections on the notions of vagary, tragedy, Clément Rosset's 'logic of the worst', *Ernstfall* and *heterotelia*.

Monnerot's Doxanalysis

In the 36th issue of *Nouvelle école*, Faye writes the following:

> What is interesting about Paretian doxanalysis [which Monnerot deciphered] is, therefore, not only its criticism of ideologies that believe themselves to be logical and neglect their own residues [which is precisely what Macronism is doing today in an emblematic fashion], but also its recognition of the fundamental invalidity of any rationalistic interpretation of the world. Behind all residues and non-logical actions lies what Jules Monnerot termed "the impulses of the human dimension".

Citing Monnerot in support of his own ideas, Faye demonstrates the fact that '*if the urges of the human dimension were completely repressed by the social aspect* [or the politically correct one, as seems to be the

---

and politicians of the African diaspora. Its purpose was to raise and foster 'Black consciousness' across Africa and its diaspora.

case today], *we would already have witnessed the bankruptcy of our species and the disappearance of the homo sapiens type that we represent*. There must therefore be a balance between residues and the various expressions of logic — this implies that it is absolutely imperative to maintain, and not eradicate, residues (considered irrational by 'political corrections'), failing which all of society would plummet into a deadly spiral. Faye's subsequent evolution — and even his slip-ups, which are nowadays considered 'involutive' by some people, in a cumbersome and heavy-going sort of way — fits into a perspective that strives to favour non-logical residues over all standstills, with the latter seen as 'worthy of the fat Demesmaeker' (to use an image that illustrates this Fayean anxiety with a caricature that would have earned his approval). In his article published in the 36th issue of *Nouvelle école*, however, he adds that a large number of residues in Europe stem from the 'Christian poison', as conceived of by Nietzsche. It is therefore necessary to replace these residues with more archaic ones drawn from classical culture or pagan European sources, a theme that would become essential in a later article on Heidegger published in the magazine's 39th issue in the autumn of 1982 and entitled '*Heidegger et la question du dépassement du christianisme*'.[12]

Once the issue on Pareto had been published in June 1981, we both set to work on another centred around Heidegger. For this instalment of *Nouvelle école*, Faye would write a long article on the Todtnauberg recluse. In the writings of the Black Forest philosopher, he would uncover a phase that he considered futuristic yet not detached from adherence to archetypes. In Heideggerian thought, which is generally categorised as being anti-technicist, Faye believed himself to have detected a 'reasoning' path that allows one to reintroduce technology into the framework of thought in a positive way, but this time, under different tables of values. Bruno V., one of Beerens' friends, was a Hellenist with a background in philosophy and had, on occasion,

---

12   TN: Heidegger and the Issue of Overcoming Christianity.

translated some important Fichte texts for various French universities. He agreed to re-read Faye's text before its publication, and although he did not agree with such an interpretation, he did not want to change one single iota of the text, since, according to his own conclusion, it retained a coherence and originality of which he, Bruno V., did not intend to deprive it. It is of course clear that Faye's interpretation of Heidegger's ideas, which was formulated in 1981, heralded all of his subsequent reflections on Archeofuturism.

At Julien Freund's Alsatian Home and the 'Closerie des Lilas' with Henri Lefebvre

The year of 1981 allowed us, furthermore, to stay in Strasbourg on two different occasions. The local G.R.E.C.E. branch was headed by Pierre Bérard, an Angevin immigrant in Alemannic and Frankish-Moselle lands, who knew nothing of Goethe's language. During a conference organised at a time when this Alsatian branch had just been launched, Faye was on the platform with Julien Freund when, suddenly, the debates were disrupted by Freddy Raphaël, the author of many books on the Jewish community of Strasbourg and of a work that had been noticed at PUF editions: 'Judaïsme et capitalisme[13]'. From the very start of the debate, Freddy Raphaël exclaimed in a most straightforward manner that 'this whole story about a "New Right" is no more than "playing with poop"', hoping, in petto, to trigger some sort of brawl. Being well-anchored in Alsatian realities and in his beloved village of Villé, which had its own Israelite community, it was Julien Freund who would finally bring him to his senses, upon which the two old companions left the conference room arm in arm to gulp down a few pints. On that day, I got the opportunity to meet some young Alsatian and German-speaking comrades, who were smitten with the work of Carl Schmitt. Later in the year, in autumn, Faye, Millau and I headed for Alsace once again to meet Julien Freund in a magnificent Alsatian

---

13   TN: Judaism and Capitalism.

inn and, following a gargantuan meal, proceeded to shoot, in the professor's home, an interview involving, on the one hand, the author of *What Is the Political?*, and, on the other, Bérard and Faye themselves. Unfortunately, due to technical reasons, the interview film turned out to be unfit for use.

The year of 1981 also provided me with a double opportunity to accompany Faye to the *Closerie des Lilas* to meet Henri Lefebvre, who had broken with the French Communist Party despite having been one of its main ideologists. I have already mentioned the profound influence that this Marxist-Leninist philosopher had on Faye,[14] a fact that should prevent some of those horrible simplifiers out there from decreeing that our friend was never anything more than a 'hick of the far-right', an insult that he was targeted with by both 'antifas' and those who, despite claiming to be his friends, would thwart all his initiatives until causing his downfall. During our meals at the *Closerie*, Lefebvre spoke of the monumental fights between rival groups that the place had witnessed during the era of Parisian surrealism. And it was Faye's 'Lefebvrism' that allowed Stefano Vaj to state in his recent homage that, just like a large number of non-dogmatic Marxists, our friend's thoughts were exclusively geared towards fostering an energising sort of revolutionary action and never perpetuating any kind of standstill, one that he readily labelled 'museographic'. In his eyes, de Benoist was, for instance, guilty of the sin of 'museography', which he committed in a most unreasonable fashion, thus causing his own thoughts to become both fragmentary and disorderly, akin to a set of scattered scraps comprised of collages and veneers, from which all pragmatic coherence vanishes in whiffs of smog that are too difficult to penetrate and, consequently, impossible to use in a genuinely metapolitical strategy, a Gramscian plan of action, etc.

Following a conference held in 1981, Faye gathered the correspondents of G.R.E.C.E. in various European countries, including

14 AN: http://robertsteuckers.blogspot.com/2011/11/influence-de-h-lefebvre-sur-g-faye.html.

Marco Tarchi and Stefano Vaj for Italy; the pontiff's deputy from the Campine/Kempen area, who had heckled him during the colloquium of June 1980 in Brussels; Michael Walker, who had just founded his own magazine, *The Scorpion*; and Pierre Krebs, who had very recently created his *Thule-Seminar*. This marked the beginning of a long cooperation, except with Tarchi and the little Campine deputy, who would obey all of the pontiff's sabotage orders like the mutts that they are. And the first one to pay the price for this would be Stefano Vaj. Faye was glad to have allowed the 'neo-rightist' endeavour to acquire a European dimension on that day — and I personally shared his joy.

The Articles of the 'Internal Report'

The S.E.R. ('Studies & Research Secretariat') was therefore Faye's prerogative in G.R.E.C.E. In the association's internal report (I.R.), which was divided into several sections comprised of loose sheets, a certain part was intended for the S.E.R. Faye published the greater part of his articles there, articles that had been excluded from the movement's major publications out of sheer jealousy, gratuitous spite, and an obscure and cruel desire to harm, reminiscent of the one that drives an evil animistic sorcerer to stick needles into wax figures representing those he wants to cast into perdition. Faye's articles could not, in fact, be published in *Nouvelle école* (where they would definitely have had a place of their own) or *Éléments*, nor even in *Études et Recherches*, a more modest publication. A secret ukase[15] had decreed this fatwa. Here is a list of Guillaume's unpublished articles, which have virtually not aged at all:

- *Qu'entendons-nous par « société marchande»?*[16] (September–October 1978);

---

15   TN: The word 'ukase' is based on a Russian term referring to a decree with the force of law issued in Tsarist Russia. In this context, however, it is to be understood as an arbitrary and dictatorial command.

16   TN: What Do We Mean by 'Mercantile Society'?

- *Géopolitique et puissance des nations*[17] (March–April 1979);

- *Analyse du* Janus *d'Arthur Koestler*[18] (March–April 1979);

- *Le commencement grec*[19] (July 1979);

- *Politique, métapolitique, parapolitique: réflexion post-gramscienne*[20] (October 1979);

- *Notre position sur l'Europe*[21] (February 1980);

- *L'économique et le politique*[22] (February 1980);

- *La puissance: une idée neuve en Europe*[23] (February 1980);

- *Réel et rationnel: peut-on concevoir un retour de la rationalité?*[24] (June–July 1980);

- *Pour une interprétation subversive du marxisme*[25] (June–July 1980);

- *Pour une sociologie de l'égalitarisme*[26] (June–July 1980);

- *Les contradictions culturelles du capitalisme*[27] (June–July 1980);

- *Qu'est-ce que la* Realpolitik?[28] (June–July 1980);

---

17 TN: Geopolitics and the Power of Nations.

18 TN: Analysis of Arthur Koestler's *Janus*.

19 TN: The Greek Beginning.

20 TN: Politics, Metapolitics, Parapolitics: A Post-Gramscian Reflection.

21 TN: Our Position Concerning Europe.

22 TN: The Economic and the Political.

23 TN: Power: A New Notion in Europe.

24 TN: The Real and the Rational: Is a Return to Rationality Possible?

25 TN: For a Subversive Interpretation of Marxism.

26 TN: For a Sociology of Egalitarianism.

27 TN: The Cultural Contradictions of Capitalism.

28 TN: What Is *Realpolitik*?

- *Les néo-conservateurs américains, exemple des contradictions internes de l'idéologie égalitaire*[29] (spring of 1981);

- *Réflexion critique sur les positions artistiques de l'école de Francfort*[30] (January–February 1981);

- *Redécouvrir Bergson*[31] (autumn of 1981);

- *La société du non-travail (I)*[32] (December 1981);

- *La société du non-travail (II)*[33] (spring of 1982).

In the I.R published in the spring of 1981, we co-authored a text entitled '*Éléments pour une théorie du politique*'.[34] In Brussels, at around the same time, the following texts by Guillaume Faye appeared in *Pour une Renaissance européenne*[35] (PURE), the G.R.E.C.E.-Belgium report that Georges Hupin was in charge of:

- *L'économie n'est pas le destin*,[36] PURE, issue number 26, March–April 1979 (an article which triggered a certain controversy with a liberal reader, André Crickx, who would then send a reader's letter that would be published in issue number 27/28, May–June–July 1979);

- *Le totalitarisme économique*,[37] PURE, issue number 32, March–April 1980;

---

29 TN: The American Neo-Conservatives: An Example of the Internal Contradictions of the Egalitarian Ideology.

30 TN: A Critical Reflection on the Artistic Positions of the Frankfurt School.

31 TN: Rediscovering Bergson.

32 TN: The Society of Non-Work I.

33 TN: The Society of Non-Work II.

34 TN: Elements for a Political Theory.

35 TN: For a European Renaissance.

36 TN: The Economy Is Not Fate.

37 TN: Economic Totalitarianism.

- *La volonté de vivre*,[38] PURE, special issue, May 1980;

- Robert Steuckers, *recension du Système à tuer les peuples de Guillaume Faye*,[39] PURE, issue number 38, summer of 1981;

- *L'Occident éclaté*,[40] PURE, issue number 39, winter of 1981.

It is all too clear: from Guillaume Faye's perspective, who was labelled a mere 'free electron'[41] on the 142nd page of an annoyingly self-glorifying work entitled *Mémoire vive*[42] (which Philippe Baillet mocks most jovially when mentioning a 'gaping memory'), this was not a bad performance at all. It also revealed the fundamentally mendacious nature of such spiteful labelling. The relevance of the above-mentioned articles and their persistent validity almost forty years later render Faye the clearest theoretician of the movement to which he once belonged and gave lustre. Lying around his office were also the remains of a rejected manuscript — that of a book on economic doctrines — inspired by List, the German historical school, Wagemann, Delaisi, Perroux, Passet and Jouvenel (on Napoleon's 'continental blockade'). I only managed to save one single meagre chapter, which would be published later in *Orientations* number 5 (1984): the manuscript itself was incomplete because, feeling disappointed, Guillaume had used some of its pages to clean his pipe... This brief chapter, saved *in extremis* from further pipe-cleaning, was entitled '*Contestation du libre-échangisme*'[43] and obviously contradicted the secret and pseudo-Machiavellian plans devised by the fairground-worthy pontiff, who, in his incredible scheming, intended to be co-opted by all Thatcherians worldwide (a topic that I shall return to!). In this same issue, I published our

---

38   TN: The Will to Live.

39   TN: A Review of Guillaume Faye's *Système à tuer les peuples*.

40   TN: A Shattered West.

41   TN: Meaning a 'free spirit'.

42   TN: A Vivid Memory.

43   TN: A Contestation of Free-Trade.

friend's theoretical and extensive study entitled *Critique du système occidental*,[44] which could still motivate today's young readers, so that they do not fall into the trap embodied by the dominant discourse, which glorifies the 'eternal values of the West or the Republic'.

The Small Lexicon of the European Partisan

During my translator's training at the Marie Haps Institute, my aesthetics and contemporary literature professor was the famous Henri Van Lier (1921–2009), who had arranged for us a file comprised of seventy-seven sheets that included new terms, generally scientific ones, heralding a new age of humanity. To Van Lier, who, at the time, was preparing his masterpiece, *Anthropogénie*[45] (which would be released in its ultimate and very extensive version in 2002), the 'Homo' species is a technician species rather than a 'speaking' one, and its 'culture' is one of tools rather than one of speech. Man's immediate action upon the material world therefore precedes speech, which is always kept at a certain distance from things (with the latter always being 'mediates'). The parallel with Arnold Gehlen is obvious here: during one of Van Lier's exams, I spoke of Gehlen, who he was still unfamiliar with, rather than the topic that was meant to be studied. Van Lier was very happy about it. Since the end of the 1970s, Gehlen had been on the 'Studies & Research Secretariat's' agenda, with Giorgio Locchi's son, Pierluigi Locchi, having devoted his graduation work to this — alas, hardly read — German sociologist and anthropologist. I myself gave a lecture on his work in 1978 as part of the circle sponsored by Georges Hupin; later, Yvan Blot would struggle to have one of Gehlen's works published at the P.U.F. Let us now, however, return to Van Lier. In his eyes, as well as those of Moeller van den Bruck prior to 1914, the distinctive architecture of a civilisation is always its starting point, the major clue that points to the beginning of a new collective human

---

44   TN: Critique of the Western System.

45   TN: Anthropogeny.

adventure. And as for the coming 'new age', it shall be a time when machines shall no longer draw their strength from man or nature, nor remain *before* man and at his disposal, but shall, instead, enter into a state of synergy *with* him and nature itself — themes that are comparable to those encountered in Jünger's '*Worker*'.

To Van Lier, who knew how to shape his own vocabulary, this was 'the 3rd age', the age of networks. The idea of putting together a file of key words, similar to Van Lier's, immediately sprang to Faye's mind: this was the origin of the *Petit lexique du partisan européen*,[46] which, having been modified and expanded upon, would give birth, in 2001, to the work *Pourquoi nous combattons*,[47] a work that was soon translated into English. It is, as everyone agrees, a genuine breviary that summarises the worldview and political outlook which Faye had always wanted to promote. However, I personally think that another volume should be added to the first file, since there are already new precursory terms present in the field of advanced sciences, especially that of biology and medicine — something that must be done now, and urgently so!

The last weeks of the spring of 1981 saw the publication of Faye's first book, *Le système à tuer les peuples*, which his own sinister sachem tried to sabotage all the way through so that the book would not be released in time for the annual conference nor compete with his own work on paganism, one that was *very*, and I mean *very*, largely inspired by the masterwork of the German philosopher and Islamologist Sigrid Hunke, *Europas wahre Religion*,[48] which had been translated by a prisoner, who had to work hard while incarcerated in order to leave something to his children, who were still studying at the time.

---

46 TN: Small Lexicon of the European Partisan.

47 TN: *Why We Fight: Manifesto of the European Resistance*, published in English by Arktos Media Ltd., 2011.

48 TN: Meaning 'Europe's True Religion', but I myself only know of Hunke's work entitled 'Europas eigene Religion', whose rendering would then be 'Europe's Own Religion'.

Faye's typescript was impeded on the grounds that it allegedly lacked bibliographic references. Sad and concerned, Faye came to my office to enquire about it. In the end, the publisher would still receive the text on time, thanks to Millau, I believe. I was actually the first to list the book for Georges Hupin's G.R.E.C.E.-Belgium report, while also reviewing the pontiff's own work, inspired by Sigrid Hunke, whose books I had read two or three years earlier, during my studies. Stefano Vaj did the same a few days later in an Italian organ.

The origin of Faye's *Système à tuer les peuples* is rooted in his speech at the Athens colloquium, which was held from 25th to 28th June, 1980 on the initiative of Jason Hadjidinas. The title given to the colloquium was 'Consciousness of Freedoms and Freedom of Conscience'. It was there that Faye presented the essential theories that would subsequently give shape to his book in 1981. His speech was entitled 'Systems Against Peoples' and was based on a reflection taken from Jürgen Habermas' *Technology and Science as Ideology*: 'Capitalist society has been transformed in such a way that it is no longer possible to directly apply two fundamental categories of Marxist theory, namely the concept of class struggle and that of ideology'. The second Colloquium of Athens would be organised on 4th and 5th October, 1982 and revolve around the topic of 'Normality'. Faye would take the floor there to talk about 'Western Ideology as a Desire for Normality'.

Jean de la Fontaine and the Old Gallic Wine

In July 1981, we hosted G.R.E.C.E.'s party conference in Roquefavour, where we welcomed Faye's faithful American friend, the solicitor Sam Dickson, who would go on the traditional hike across the crests of the Lubéron in dress shoes, thus literally destroying his fine soles and damaging his footwear's leather, which made him look like the English prisoners who, in a well-known cult film, enter the prison camp of *The Bridge of the River Kwai* while whistling a tune once famous across the Channel. Stefano Vaj, who had come from Milan, was also among us.

The atmosphere was thunderous. In the evening, once our work was done, Faye recited his colourful and naughty versions of La Fontaine's fables and sang his favourite song, 'Le vieux vin gaulois',[49] in a loud voice.

In 1981, we were fortunately able to perfect our work in offices where only low-ranked staff was active, overwhelmed by ideological issues. Indeed, the organisation's sinister pontiff disappeared on a regular basis without offering any explanations or giving instructions. In July, following a meeting of the editorial secretariat, he vanished for a period of seven weeks under the pretext of travelling to the Far East to cover a story for *Le spectacle du monde* magazine, passing through California, USA on the way back, where the sister of a female friend of his, who had come along to indulge his whims, apparently studied (somewhere around Las Vegas — who knows what exactly!). He simply had to go and shake the young damsel's hand, while simultaneously emulating, albeit in less time, the feat accomplished by Phileas Fogg, Jules Verne's famous hero. At the end of September, he would announce that he was going to the Frankfurt Fair, as he always did, year in, year out. Although the fair in question only lasts for five days, he would actually return three weeks later! Before disappearing again at the end of November, convinced that some thugs wanted to assassinate him: he is said to have holed up in a shabby hotel, shut-away in a small room and armed with a shot gun — he would resurface fifteen days later in an appalling state, giving off an atrocious stench, having seen no soap, polish or toothpaste during his voluntary exile in this half-dilapidated hovel. And three minutes after his odorous return, he actually had the audacity to scold us both, Faye and me, and shout: 'It's like *Zig et Puce*[50] in here! It's the Marx Brothers!' Faye got a lot of grief. On that day, my convictions were set — I decided to get the

---

49 TN: The Old Gallic Wine.

50 TN: 'Zig et Puce' (i.e. Zig and Puce) is a Franco-Belgian comics series created by Alain Saint-Ogan in 1925; it enjoyed huge popularity and exerted great social influence over a long period of time. In this context, Alain de Benoist

hell out of there. How is one to work coherently and abide by any sort of agenda when one's leader — who always insists on approving every single thing and the slightest detail — is constantly somewhere out, enjoying himself, or in a state of depression (depressions which were, above all else, staged and utterly tasteless acts of deception)? How can one, in fact, serve such a character without looking at oneself in the mirror? My discovery of some of our fairground sachem's (highly unhygienic) quirks only served to reinforce my decision to leave once and for all. A fortnight later, I asked Millau to pay me my wages and be kind enough to accept my resignation.

Faye, the Guarantor of Serious Metapolitics

In such a context, contrary to what one might believe today in the aftermath of Faye's Skyrock radio adventures and his numerous jokes and good subversive pranks on both the *Place de Paris* and elsewhere, ideological seriousness was on his side, and his side alone. First of all, throughout the year of 1981, he had hindered all the potential follies on the part of the movement's silly pope, who intended to be the only one calling the shots inside the headquarters located on *rue Charles-Lecocq* and hoped to be given a blank check by everyone else to indulge all of his incongruous whims and 'paganistic helpings dipped in Nazis-tika sauce'. One day, this plastic tiara-crowned pope declared to me, with the seriousness of a Presbyterian undertaker, that he wanted to follow up on the issue we had published on Pareto with another on the topic of Atlantis; a topic which, at the time, was in vogue in a vaguely sectarian and orgy-loving socialite network known as the 'Nouvelle Acropole',[51] in which he had some truly bizarre friends! When I shared this with Faye, he obviously tapped his forehead with his index finger and felt genuinely sorry — one could feel that he had been profoundly

---

mentioned it metaphorically to allude to the messy and chaotic conditions which, according to him, had spread during his absence.

51   TN: New Acropole.

afflicted by this, because he knew that owing to such barren whims, the movement was in danger of being assimilated to a sect of eccentrics and losing all the good contacts it maintained with high-level academics; and what Faye wanted to avoid above all was being yelled at by Julien Freund. A day later, I heard some screams coming from Faye's office and a door being violently slammed. Intrigued, I went to see what was happening. What I found was a dumbstruck and slightly trembling Guillaume: just above his head was a paper knife embedded in the wall. The guru had come to pay him a visit and stubbornly insisted, with the whiny fury of a spoilt child, on having his absurd idea of publishing an issue on Atlantis accepted; to which Faye had immediately replied: 'And why not release an issue on the lost continent of Mu?'. Furious at his reply, the guru had grabbed a paper knife and hurled it straight into the wall behind Faye.

In the evening, I used a typewriter (a more sophisticated model than the one that had been entrusted to me) located in the secretary's large office, taking advantage of the fact that she had returned home to cook her vespertine grub. The guru-pope then spoke to me and reminded me about his outlandish project: I resisted his idea with the same obstinacy as Faye's, suggesting, instead, an issue that would be entitled 'Archaeology of the North Sea' (for the pontiff believed Atlantis to be situated in the vicinity of Heligoland). Throwing a new tantrum worthy of Louis de Funès films, he grabbed another letter opener and propelled it, in a display of remarkable dexterity, into a small cork-cased alarm clock in front of me. With the calmness of a Coldstream Guard in his sentry box at Buckingham, I reiterated my refusal, upon which he left the premises, grumbling and annoyed at the fact that no one was willing to indulge his whims. I thought to myself: if this bloke were to go into exile someday, he would do what General Alcazar ends up doing in *The Seven Crystal Balls*:[52] he would become a dagger thrower in some cheap music hall. This comparison

---

52   TN: *The Seven Crystal Balls* is the 13th volume of the Adventures of Tintin.

made Faye laugh. The moral of this ludicrous story is that it was crucial not to include the word 'Atlantis' on the cover of the magazine if one still desired to be taken seriously. Faye had been right all along. In August, however, at a time when the *pontifexminimus* was wandering around, enjoying the sautéed rice of Singapore, Hollywood burgers and the rillettes[53] prepared by the two damsels, I went to both Denmark and Schleswig-Holstein in order to collect archaeological documentation (especially at the North Frisian Institute of Bredstedt and with the help of archaeologist Jürgen Spanuth) and meet the Scandinavist and *Nouvelle école* correspondent in Germany François-Xavier Dillmann and the sociologist Henning Eichberg at a 'folk high school' in Tinglev. I thus attempted, at Faye's request, to 'scientificate' the whims of the great *panjandrum*, who would have an issue published on the topic a few years later — it would be titled 'Archaeology'. Phew!

The Bad Joke of a 'Liberal Alternative'

Worse was, however, to come during this autumn of 1981: going behind everyone's back and taking advantage of his position at *Le Figaro Magazine*, the manitou of Prisunic stores was planning to stand on the rostrum of a symposium that he himself would organise, thanks to some dummy corporations and an *ad hoc* association, whose headquarters were located in the apartment of his poor late mother, who had just passed away in June. This conference was announced under the heading of 'Liberal Alternative' and would attract the entire Thatcherian and Reaganian neoliberalist high society to Paris, an essentially Anglo-Saxon Areopagus amidst which we were going to advertise our soppy Sagamore as being a little prodigy, whose thoughts were going to save our poor France from the clutches of the wicked social-statist Mitterrandism that had been engulfing it since the elections of May 1981. To Faye, who was in favour of a guided economy, an

---

53   TN: Potted meat.

interventionistic one in terms of infrastructure and heterodox in the sense of taking into account non-economic factors (in contrast with Marxian, liberal and Keynesian orthodoxies), this attempt to align oneself with Reaganism seemed to be a completely preposterous idea or, worse, an outright betrayal of our fundamental Europeanist message. Retrospectively, this reckless entryism proved that Locchi had been right to bow out two years earlier. At the time, Faye was an attentive reader of the economist André Grjébine, who had authored *La nouvelle économie internationale*,[54] published by P.U.F. back in 1980. Grjébine championed a self-sufficient, semi-autarkic European continent. I obviously shared this point of view, as did Angel Sampieru, who was a Parisian G.R.E.C.E. activist at the time, and the entire team that had remained in Brussels and Liège and whose members were my friends. The great bigwig-polygraph had prepared his coup by writing dithyrambic articles on Raymond Aron (who had been invited to the colloquium) and Karl Popper (whose main disciples, hostile to any sort of 'closed society', were to step up to the rostrum and debate their neoliberal nonsense around his august person) before publishing them in *The Fig' Mag'*. Alas for him, the Parousia's advent was not to be immediate: the statal and diasporic services quickly became aware of the oh-so-easy-to-see-through little scheme devised by our little pantomimic Machiavelli. And thus was the intruder-ousting machine set off: Aron refused to speak as long as our Atlantean doxographer from the 6th arrondissement was present at the colloquium, while others threatened to resign. He was basically driven out of his own theatre, so to speak. The impervious depression he fell into in November 1981 can indeed be explained by this resounding defeat. Note that one had to be utterly unrealistic, and with a pedigree such as his, to ever have believed, even if only for an instant, that such a concoction could ever lead to success! Unless his very recent reconciliation with Finkielkraut and Minc and, in March of 2019, the speech he delivered on the

---

54   TN: A New International Economy.

rostrum of a certain braggart (who is now based in Brussels and continues to loudly advertise our good city among our exiled and taxable French candidates) are actually the desired result of a fundamental and almost genetic type of liberalism, which, for obscure reasons, had been concealed behind other forms of discourse, including anti-liberal ones. For he has continuously maintained ambiguities, accumulated contradictions, and ejected all proponents of genuine economic heterodoxy: one thus rightfully wonders about things and asks questions, which, in any case, the analysts of this (allegedly 'new-rightist') movement are bound to ask themselves in future. Their conclusions will, however, undoubtedly point to the complete inconsistency displayed by the doxographer, whose cranial cavity is home to genuine chaotic confusion and whose strategy is restricted to staging coups so as to ease his own progress. Faye's appraisals in this regard can therefore be said to have been premonitory.

The failure of the concoction and the ejection of the aggrieved great wizard would first trigger a terrible depression in him and then a vengeful and spiteful fit of rage, increased tenfold by the fact that he had now been kicked out of the editorial staff of *Fig' Mag'*, except for one miserable little column on the topic of videos, which Louis Pauwels, ever a kindly soul, allowed him to keep in a display of great magnanimity. What this rage would dictate upon him was a new national-revolutionary orientation, which would immediately be expressed on the pages of *Éléments* and claim our adhesion. The bloke had saved his own shop: one forgot the fruitless mistakes he had made during the autumn of 1981 and thought that everything had gone back to normal, since he now seemed to profess a radically anti-Westernist sort of Europeanism. I left Paris in December 1981 and, in the course of 1982, participated in a general assembly organised by G.R.E.C.E. in Lyon, before giving a lecture at the 'Cercle Héraclite', a lecture that dealt with German national neutrality and was hostile to the placement of American missiles on the territory of the FRG. This position made it possible for us to establish links with other political movements located in many European countries. The internal report devoted a few pages to this topic, which, at the time, was something entirely new in the movement. In October 1982, I began my ten-months of military service in Saive, near Liège, before moving on to Marche-en-Famenne, Bürvenich and Vogelsang in the Eifel region. During my training period, Faye announced that he would hold a seminar organised by a new structure on the premises in *rue Blanche*, in the ninth arrondissement. This seminar, which was followed by a second one a few months later (in 1983), was, in my eyes, the pinnacle of Faye's metapolitical work.

The Rue Blanche Seminars

During these two seminars, Faye proceeded to gather around himself such luminaries as Stéphane Lupasco, Bassarab Nicolescu, Manuel de Diéguez, Jules Monnerot and various supporters of his ideas, which included Professors Martinez, Wagner and Asso. The lectures followed one another in a joyous and relaxed atmosphere, without the psychological stiffness which the pontiff systematically gener-ated around himself, passing on his internal stress and anxieties to the public. Unfortunately, no written record of these seminars has survived, as Faye lacked the means to have the speech texts printed in the form of a single volume: indeed, the financial windfalls had to flow exclusively towards a certain purse and were, above all else, not to be devoted to any valid and fruitful metapolitical endeavours. It was during these seminars that I had the opportunity to speak to Jules Monnerot, who was very pleased with Faye's article on his conception of doxanalysis, and to enjoy the words of praise uttered by Manuel de Diéguez, who had appreciated my articles in *Nouvelle école*. Next in line was Hebdo Magazine, which began to be published in 1983 and where Faye, under the pseudonym of Gérald Fouchet, was in charge of compiling the weekly's most important interviews. Once again, he shone most brightly. Religiously, I kept this collection of interviews, which would later be published in one single volume (following the magazine's bankruptcy), but, alas, under a third party's name, one that probably cashed in on the copyrights… And yet Faye had displayed highly professional know-how when putting together these many interviews.

From 1983 to 1986, Faye did not stop publishing brochures. He was, incidentally, not allowed to do more than that. One wanted to limit him as much as possible and make him a man that had only penned one single book, one that had already been forgotten or gone out of print: *Le système à tuer les peuples*, released back in 1981. Next to be published was a series of brief but thick brochures such as: *Contre l'économisme* (1983), of which I had to publish a second makeshift edition because Faye had been refused a second print run; *Sexe and idéologie*[55] (1983), a small and modest pamphlet that would nonetheless serve as basis for his major work of 2011, *Sexe et dévoiement*,[56] published by Lore editions and then quickly translated into English (it is currently a best-selling volume in a series of translations released by Arktos Media Ltd.); *La nouvelle société de consommation*[57] (1984); and *L'Occident comme déclin*[58] (1984), an excellent text, whose manuscript was categorically rejected but funded by our friend Patrice Sage and then, in its second edition, by my Eurograf friends in Liège, who signed a proper contract with Faye — to which the pontiff's henchmen responded most swiftly, as some meaningless little solicitor proceeded to threaten me through the phone. A few days later, he would be dismissed and then ridiculed by a Languedoc solicitor during the G.R.E.C.E. symposium held in *Pavillon Baltard*. Faye faced a terrible dilemma in 1985: it was impossible to find such a generous donor as Patrice Sage (who obviously did not have inexhaustible funds) for

---

55   TN: Sex and Ideology.

56   TN: *Sex and Deviance*, published by Arktos Media Ltd. in 2014.

57   TN: The New Consumerist Society.

58   TN: The West as an Embodiment of Decline.

each and every volume he wrote. I thus appealed to my Eurograf friends, including the late Jean-Marie Simar, who successively published, in addition to the second edition of *L'Occident comme déclin*, the *Europe et modernité*[59] brochure and the first version of *Petit lexique du partisan européen*, which would enjoy remarkable success thanks to the emergence of several pirated editions (whose publications would stretch until the threshold of the 2000s). In *Orientations* (issue number 5, August–September 1984), I would first publish the theoretical essay entitled *Critique du système occidental* and then two solid studies, namely *Les néo-conservateurs américains, exemple des contradictions internes de l'idéologie égalitaire* and *À la découverte de Thorstein Veblen*[60] (*Orientations*, issue number 6, September–October 1985), both of which were taken from our I.R.'s old S.E.R. notebooks, i.e. from the ultra-confidential publication that served as a kind of purgatory to Faye, whose texts were mostly rejected. Yet Faye managed to keep *Élements* at arm's length while still ensuring that the magazine, whose topics he chose, did not change course.

L'Occident comme déclin remains, in my eyes, one of the best texts Faye ever penned. Judge by the chapter titles yourselves: *Cosmopolis: l'Occident comme non-lieu;*[61] *Fin de l'idéologie ou idéologie de la fin?;*[62] *Christopolis: l'Occident comme athéisme chrétien;*[63] *Antipolis ou la fin du politique;*[64] and so on. *Europe et modernité* heralds most clearly Faye's Archeofuturistic ideas with chapters such as: *L'hypothèse de*

---

59   TN: Europe and Modernity.

60   TN: Discovering Thorstein Veblen.

61   TN: Cosmopolis — The West: Case Dismissed.

62   TN: The End of Ideology or The Ideology of the End?

63   TN: Christopolis: The West as the Embodiment of Christian Atheism.

64   TN: Antipolis or the End of the Political.

l'inconscient pré-néolithique;[65] *L'hypothèse de l'inconscient païen;*[66] *L'échec de la nouvelle conscience et de la première modernité;*[67] etc.

Faye, the Driving Force Behind *Élements* Magazine

Let us now return to Guillaume Faye's role in the columns of the New Right's/*Canal historique*'s[68] primary magazine. Very young, very child-like and his face covered by a huge pair of glasses, he had already appeared in a photo published in November/December 1973 as part of the magazine's second issue, alongside Michel Droit, who, just like Faye himself, had participated in G.R.E.C.E.'s ninth national conference of 21st October, 1973, together with Pierre Garrigue, Michel Mourlet, Jean Cau and Giorgio Locchi. He was presented as a 'member of the National Secretariat of G.R.E.C.E.' — and yet, he would later be labelled, I remind you, as a 'free electron' that one did not remember too well… It was not until the 8th–9th issue of *Élements* that one encountered a very brief article by Faye on 'The Third World Church', an article that has no polemical aspects yet gives a smooth assessment of the 'theology of revolutionary practice' in the aftermath of a synod held in Rome in October 1974.

One would have to wait until the 28th–29th issue of March 1979 to see him reappear in the columns of the magazine, where a solid file on 'totalitarian economy' — or rather totalitarian 'economicism', G.R.E.C.E.'s hobby horse at the time — was published, mainly at Faye's instigation. One can easily guess that he himself was actually the editor of the summary report entitled *Économie organique et société marchande.*[69] It was he who penned *La dictature du bien-être,*[70] where

---

65   TN: The Theory of a Pre-Neolithic Unconscious.

66   TN: The Theory of a Pagan Unconscious.

67   TN: The Failure of the New Consciousness and of the First Modernity.

68   TN: Historical Channel.

69   TN: Organic Economy and Mercantile Society.

70   TN: The Dictatorship of Well-Being.

one already encounters the pontiff's current shifts towards the feelings that drove Marx to write his 'Manifesto of the Communist Party' (1848). In this very same issue, one notices the inclusion (by Faye) of an interview with Julien Freund, the first step in a long-lasting collaboration between the two men. It must be said that I, too, aligned myself spontaneously with these economic and political theories, for Freund's following words had become embedded in my brain: '*The common mistake of liberalism and Marxism consists in making economic rationality the model of all rationality (…). Indeed, the worst sort of irrationality is to think that one could ever rationalise everything*'.

Faye only reappeared in the 33ʳᵈ issue (February/March 1980), where he briefly spoke of a trip with his friends to Greece. The 34ᵗʰ issue (dated April/May 1980) established him, once and for all, as the editorial staff's driving force. Entitled *Pour en finir avec la civilisation occidentale* and released after the *Nouvelle école* issue devoted to America (1975), it marked the beginning of the New Right's anti-Westernist and Spengler-tinged turning point: the current US-centred West is merely a civilisation and not a culture anymore, experiencing an ultimate and stagnant stage and no longer one of youth and natural creativity. In his own way, Faye resorts to the term 'Hesperia' once used by Heidegger, a choice which he explains in an insert bearing the title *Quand l'Occident a oublié la Grèce.*[71] Criticising the new 'human rights' craze in the same vein, Faye returned in issue 37 (January–March 1981): he co-authored, alongside Alain de Benoist, a long article entitled *La religion des droits de l'Homme*[72] and penned, all alone, the section's two other articles: *Genèse d'une idéologie*[73] and *Le droit des hommes.*[74] In the 38ᵗʰ issue (spring 1981), he mentioned

---

71   TN: When the West Has Forgotten Greece.

72   TN: The Religion of Human Rights.

73   TN: The Genesis of an Ideology.

74   TN: The Right of Men.

Alain de Benoist's book entitled *Comment peut-on être païen?*.[75] In issue number 39 (summer 1981), Faye and I co-authored *La leçon de Carl Schmitt*.[76] Next, in the 41st issue (March–April 1982), he analysed Konrad Lorenz's *L'Homme dans le fleuve du vivant*.[77] In issue number 42 (June–July 1982), he was excluded from the major section devoted to socialism, as dictated by the pontiff's post-Thatcherian reorientation, yet still authored an article that has almost not aged at all: *Pour l'indépendance économique*,[78] a text based on two major works of the era, which were overshadowed by the wave of triumphant neoliberalism: *La nouvelle politique internationale*[79] by André Grjébine and *Pour une économie du nouveau développement*[80] by François Perroux. These are the works that Faye had read the previous year but whose publication had been rejected, since it was necessary, back then, to accommodate all types of Thatchero-Reaganians, who were subsidised by the American caucuses. The failure of the 'Liberal Alternative' project in December 1981 had proved Faye right and enabled, within the ranks of the NR, the triumph of the ideological-economic vein of heterodoxy, a vast intellectual continent that emphasises the existence of specific and inalienable contexts and postulates different economic paces and practices each and every time, with the impossibility of reducing them to any common denominator. The economy must therefore free itself from all reductionist projects, which rationalise things to the point of absurdity, de-contextualise and stubbornly reject any anthropological nuances. Regulation, postulated by every genuinely political economy,

---

75 TN: How Can One Be Pagan?

76 TN: Carl Schmitt's Lesson.

77 TN: Literally 'Man in the River of the Living'. I have researched things most extensively and concluded that the work in question is a French translation of '*Das Wirkungsgefüge der Natur und das Schicksal des Menschen*', i.e. The Structure of Nature and the Fate of Man.

78 TN: For Economic Independence.

79 TN: The New International Policy.

80 TN: For an Economy of New Development.

must thus not operate on the basis of rigid and repetitive codes *ad infinitum*, but must, instead, be modulated in accordance with specific contexts and anthropologies, failing which it would plummet into Orwellian totalitarianism or permanent and absurd judicial repression worthy of the 'politically correct', as witnessed every day. Inquisitorial repression has advanced hand in hand with neoliberalism, which has, ever so hypocritically, proclaimed a return to freedom!

Youth and the State

As part of the *La fin de la jeunesse*[81] section in the 43rd issue (October/ November 1982), Faye authored an article, which he titled *Les héros sont fatigués*.[82] This is what he wrote there:

> The events are unfolding as if [...] social ideology had created a sham of youth and incarcerated it in an artificial world in order to prevent youths from genuinely revolting.

All of Faye's rebellious personality is summed up in this seemingly innocuous yet astute sentence. Faye sensed and felt, and very clearly so, the heavy shackles of false youthfulness that gradually imprisoned the new generations. At least three of them had already experienced this deleterious and suffocating 'stranglehold confinement'. You can actually see the results today by simply leaning against your balcony's handrail and watching passers-by. The 44th issue (January/February 1983) was devoted to the topic of the state. Although Faye co-authored the main article, *Contre l'État-Providence*,[83] as well as another, *Pour un État souverain*,[84] with Alain de Benoist, he was obviously the main source of inspiration and editor. It was he who, all alone, wrote *Le*

---

81   TN: The End of Youth.

82   TN: The Heroes Are Tired.

83   TN: Against the Welfare State.

84   TN: For a Sovereign State.

libéralisme, ça ne marche pas.[85] In this text, which is still very useful to read and ponder today, he states:

> To re-establish the truth is to affirm that a private, competitive and dynamic economy can only be a national one that has been placed under the state's motivating and protecting governance, and that it is, in fact, liberalism which can ruin it by systematically favouring financial institutions and multinational monopolistic companies.

None can deny the fact that this conclusion was truly prophetic! In issue number 45 (Spring 1983), Faye pays tribute to one of his favourite contemporary philosophers, Jean Baudrillard (*La stratégie Baudrillard*[86]). The text is an analysis of *Les stratégies fatales*,[87] which had, at the time, been published by Grasset. What Faye had noted in his idol's last book was a shift towards 'ad-ideology', yet still highlighted the work's solid core: one must rid oneself of the pathos of modernity, i.e. of the ideology of liberation and communication, of the massifying and narcissism-bearing universal passion for love and replace it with an enticement that is 'controversial, intensity-generating and twofold', in order to overcome the age of disenchantment once announced by Max Weber.

Gadget Culture and Postmodernity

Released in the summer of 1983, the 46th issue was devoted to 'gadget culture' and was intended to serve as a response to the cultural policy embraced by the then minister, Jack Lang. In his main article, however, Faye goes further and analyses in depth the eternal relationship between culture and politics. He thus concludes:

> A cultural policy will only become possible once it has been agreed that the state, first of all, and the people, secondly, can once again exert

---

85   TN: Liberalism Does Not Work.

86   TN: The Baudrillard Strategy.

87   TN: Fatal Strategies.

influence upon culture; i.e. when, in all fields simultaneously, including the economic, geopolitical and military one, European nations manage to free themselves from the clutches of the mechanisms that relate to American-Western civilisation. A cultural policy will, likewise, become possible once more when the conception of culture inherited from the Enlightenment and liberalism has been relinquished; when, in the values scale espoused by both rulers and peoples, independence and survival are, above all else, measured in relation to *cultural identity*.

Yet another blatancy that our contemporaries fail to see! The 47th issue (autumn 1983) was devoted to the topic of 'intellectual vacuum'. Once again, the lead article was penned by Faye himself. In contrast with Armin Mohler, who, in the columns of the German magazine *Criticon*, had pinned his hopes on postmodernity, which he regarded as the ultimate transcendence of the shortcomings of liberal modernity, Faye followed in his footsteps but made a different observation, one that had a more pessimistic connotation that would ultimately prove correct:

> If post-modern periods do, in fact, exist and are not an optical illusion (which is, unfortunately, equally possible), then they occur *in the aftermath* of egalitarian (or inegalitarian) progressivist modernity, *not* in contrast with it.

In a second article entitled '*Totalitarisme et culture*',[88] he strived to re-assert the importance of the role played by the Prince, who directs the actions of the artist that constructs the living decor, the true essence of the artist's dream. There is no great art but that which is supported by a 'Great Policy'; '*which neither totalitarian shams nor, a fortiori, liberal illusions have been able to accomplish*'. These last two issues of *Élements* truly established Faye's indisputable authority over the magazine itself and, as a result, over the positive ideological shifts of the neo-rightist movement. This development would cause his downfall: the 'men of lesser worth' (to use the expression coined by Edgar Julius Jung), who

---

88   TN: Totalitarianism and Culture.

had hitherto only vegetated in his proximity, would, with the pontiff at the forefront, initiate the process that would lead to his ejection.

Fundamental Authors

The 48th–49th issue (winter 1983/1984) was devoted to the topic of 'Third-Worldism and the Cause of Peoples'. Faye had been excluded from the main section, a section that had been entirely 'phagocytosed' by the pontiff himself, who intended to reclaim his virtuousness and rid himself of the 'racialist' label, which the establishment's vigilantes had systematically been stamping him with. Faye withdrew so as to focus on a useful task — that of re-emphasising not only the movement's fundamental works and authors, but also those of any political culture. In this 48th–49th issue, he would tackle three of them, though only from page 53 onwards: he would first discuss Pierre Debray-Ritzen and Rougier, and then, on page 69, at the very back of the issue, what would later become, in the aftermath of his double eviction, his major and almost unique theme: *La société multiraciale en question*.[89] In it, he articulated his arguments in a significantly different manner from that which would characterise his later works, yet this main article does indeed deserve to be re-read, especially by those who speak of 're-migration'. The central theme of the 50th issue (Spring / Summer 1984) would be 'Money'. In his article entitled *'La fin du bas de laine'*,[90] he developed a very complex theory on the relationship between money and civilisation, in which he mentioned 'Michael Jackson, the American singer'. He then went on to explore the movement's philosophical fundamentals by re-examining Konrad Lorenz's work entitled 'The Foundations of Ethology'. In issue number 51 (autumn 1984), which centred around the topic of 'European myths', he restricted

---

89   TN: Calling the Multiracial Society into Question.

90   TN: The Drying Up of the Nest Egg.

himself to publishing two brief articles on America: '*L'Amérique mène la danse*'[91] and '*Californie, ça suffit!*'.[92]

As for the 52nd issue (January/February 1985), its topic was 'Democracy: An Instruction Manual'. Faye only authored one single article in it, entitled '*Peut-on encore être démocate?*',[93] in which he wrote the following sentence:

> The crucial issue faced by those who represent the general will is *cultural rather than institutional*. "Good constitutions" (including that of the Fifth Republic) are, of course, both necessary and essential, yet they remain insufficient. For they can be neutralised, as is the case today, by a *sociological* evolution, which, for instance, only drives the mediocre to run for office or establishes, within the nation, uncontrolled powers wielded by corporations and private factions.

How premonitory! The 53rd issue (Spring 1985), in turn, focused on the topic of 'Arabs' and the possibilities of a strategic alliance between Europeans and the Arabic-speaking peoples of the Mediterranean basin. It was Faye who authored the lead article, which acted as a prelude to the Euro-Arab colloquium of Mons (see below) and was entitled '*Pour une alliance euro-arabe*'.[94] Although this may seem paradoxical when one considers Faye's subsequent writings, let us not forget that we were in an entirely different situation back in the 1980s: indeed, the Algerian and/or Egyptian military regimes had not been weakened by the Salafists and the Muslim Brotherhood, who were ultimately controlled by the American and/or British services. Algerian diplomacy, in fact, resolved many problems in the Arab-Muslim world. Bourguiba, a nationalist, remained in the saddle in Tunis. As for Turkey, it was still Kemalist. Hafez al-Assad's Syria had stood firm against the revolution fomented by the Muslim Brotherhood in 1981.

---

91   TN: America Leads the Dance.

92   TN: Enough, California!

93   TN: Can One Still Be a Democrat?

94   TN: For a Euro-Arab Alliance.

On his side, Gaddafi was deploying his original political system. All were valid interlocutors, all the more so since *perestroika* announced an inevitable withdrawal of the Soviet bloc, with which dialogue was also becoming possible. Many of the hopes that emerged in the 1980s were to be shattered in the 1990s and 2000s. In issue number 54/55 (summer 1985), Faye wrote another article that anticipated his latest views by a period of almost twenty years: '*Contre la société multiraciale*',[95] which advocated a Euro-Maghrebi policy of migrational regulation.

A Prophetic Note

The 56th issue centred around the 'Eighteen Springs of the New Right'. Faye was kept out of the entire section, save for one beautiful and uncaptioned photo. He did, however, author a long analysis of General Baron Jordis von Lohausen's geopolitical book entitled *Mut zur Macht: Denken in Kontinenten*,[96] which was published in French by éditions du Labyrinthe. In issue number 57–58 (spring 1986), the editorial team dealt with the topic of Russia ('*Russie: le dernier empire?*'[97]). Faye, who was already half-ousted at the time, did not contribute to the section, but penned a review of a book entitled *L'éclipse du sacré*,[98] co-authored by Alain de Benoist and Thomas Molnar. In the 60th issue, Faye would write his last article in *Élements* — a methodical analysis of Guy Hocquenghem's pamphlet that bore the title *Lettre ouverte à ceux qui sont passé du col Mao au Rotary*.[99] In it, Hocquenghem castigates the old sixty-eighters that have now 're-focused their lives on modernity'. Faye concludes: we shall all bear witness to former-leftists endorsing

---

95   TN: Against a Multiracial Society.

96   TN: The Courage to Claim Power: Thinking in Terms of Continents.

97   TN: Russia: The Last Empire?

98   TN: Eclipse of the Sacred.

99   TN: Open Letter to Those That Have Discarded Their Mandarin Collars to Join Rotary International.

CRS[100] interventions, organising symposiums in support of the West and NATO, and perhaps even calling the army to the rescue so as to subdue those that would rebel. That is precisely how far things have gone with regard to the 'yellow vests'... And it was on this prophetic note that Faye ceased to write for *Élements*.

Gilbert Durand's Questionnaire

On 27th November, 1984, Gilbert Durand, a specialist in religious matters and the future host of 'Religiological' in Canada, wrote to Guillaume Faye from Savoy and provided him with a questionnaire intended for the principal leaders of the New Right, in order to be able to define their conception of the religious. On 5th December, 1984, Faye sent the questionnaire to his friends, asking them to send him their reactions and responses very soon. Immediately afterwards, and on the same day, he wrote to the venerable and sympathetic professor, pointing out to him that the NR's approach, which Durand criticised, basically aimed to reach the same goal as he himself did in his research, in particular with regard to 'blind and naive faith', i.e. the fact of 'preventing the impairment of the imagination': in order to attain this, Durand had chosen a non-technicist path, one of returning to telluric carnality in a predominantly Catholic setting, while Faye had opted for a technicist's imagination linked to an archaic and pre-Christian one (in a prelude to his 'Archeofuturism'). He furthermore promised to answer the professor's 'socio-political' questions, which were more relevant to current affairs. The pontiff would sabotage the initiative, declaring to his interlocutors, including myself, that the initiative had been terminated. I had started to respond to the questionnaire, as had others, no doubt, including Vial, Bérard and Bouts. I had not completed the task and still regret it, even after almost forty years. It

---

100 TN: The CRS (*Companies républicaines de sécurité*) are the general reserve of the French police force. What they are most famous for is their role in crowd and riot control.

was all yet another act of sabotage due to the pathological jealousy of a professional swaggerer and to his genuine dread of not being able to cut the mustard or having Faye rob him of some imaginary authority, when Durand had actually asked for spontaneous answers, answers that were not necessarily structured in a manner befitting Aristotelian, Kantian, Hegelian or Heideggerian philosophy; for a person's religious disposition is obviously not the product of some hyper-logical reasoning or flamboyant set of syllogisms.

The Forgotten Articles of '*Le Lien*'

In the period that followed my departure in December 1981 and preceded his own (at the end of 1986), Faye's new tasks included the regular production of a newsletter entitled *Le Lien*, which had taken over from the I.R., generally more elaborate but less frequently published. Considering the fact that he was no more than a 'free electron' that was alleged to have only stealthily passed through the corridors of the New Right's committee rooms (*Canal historique*), and someone who, it would seem, is only vaguely remembered by the pontiff because 'he was not a friend', as he declared in Paris a few days after Faye's passing, this work, combined with other tasks and constant public speeches throughout France and elsewhere, was anything but negligible. In the 41st issue (of 17th February, 1983), he thus compiled a section entitled 'Bibliographic News' because, as he himself stated in the introduction, '*ten years ago, when we strode along the shelves of bookstores, very few new books seemed to concern us in any way. [...] Today, [...] our contemporaries' reflection scopes cover an ever-increasing number of our concerns*'. He then went on to add:

> This remark is a capital one: our thought current managed to foresee the problems of our age before anyone else could.

Faye criticised Emmanuel Todd's *La troisième planète*[101] with regard to the relationships between family structures and ideological systems, as well as Zeev Sternhell's *Ni droite ni gauche*;[102] Philippe Beneton's *Le fléau du bien*,[103] Jean Baudrillard's *Stratégies fatales*, *The Joyless Society* by the German filmmaker Syberberg, and others. These books remain significant in this second decade of the 21st century and are now regarded as thought classics. Faye had both flair and intuition, more so than any one of us, and certainly more than the pontiff himself.

The 55th issue (of 19th October, 1983) mentions the colloquium of Athens and Cyprus sponsored by Jason Hadjidinas (see above), where Faye and Bérard also took the floor with Lucien Sfez, Michel Maffesoli and Robert Muchembled, among other prominent figures of the French teaching system. Faye declared that this conference was the continuation of and the prelude to the seminar of his own network, '*Collectif de Recherches sur le monde contemporain*'.[104] The 57th issue (of 17th November, 1983) mentions Guillaume Faye's lecture tour across the Minervois territory, on the initiative of the 'Cercle Marc-Aurèle'[105] chaired by Doctor Morell, to talk about the NR's economic proposals — this would give rise to three articles published in the local popular dailies, namely *La Dépêche du Midi*, *L'indépendant de Carcassonne* and *Le Midi Libre*, all of which were dated 20th October, 1983. The 58th issue (16th December, 1983) refers to a colloquium held on the 9th of December of the same year in Montpellier on the initiative of Professor Pierre Debray-Ritzen and entitled '*Forum Psychiatries et société*',[106] where Faye spoke on the topic of '*Freud and Keynes: The Dominant Economy as a Source of Therapy and Normalisation*'. In 1984, *Le Lien*

---

101 TN: The Third Planet.

102 TN: Neither the Right nor the Left.

103 TN: The Plague of Good.

104 TN: Collective of Research on the Contemporary World.

105 TN: The Marcus Aurelius Circle.

106 TN: The Psychiatry and Society Forum.

underwent a change in numbering, and it was the 1st issue of 1st March, 1984 that undoubtedly contained *the* precursory article that heralded Faye's future anti-immigration positions: '*Orientation/l'immigration: notre position*'.[107] The 21st issue of January 1986 included an editorial run by Faye himself and entitled '*Troisième ou seconde voie?*',[108] a text which is now undoubtedly dated, as the period of hope inaugurated by Gorbachev's *perestroika* has since evaporated — and a long time ago, at that. Faye's article, on the other hand, published at the end of the report and entitled '*La femme maîtrise-t-elle son image?*',[109] is always worth the reader's time. Faye writes:

> The image of the "current woman" derives from the sickly mythology spread by the American feminist movements of the 1960s, but also from the pseudo-feminine ideal-types of the "Parisian-sexy-intellectual", conveyed, since the start of the post-war period, by a sub-intelligentsia that belongs to the left-hand side of the political spectrum — a bastard mixture of a bogus star and a restaurant diva with the added look of a "press secretary" or "public relations specialist".

It is a text that deserves to be re-read, especially today, when feminism is reactivating its delusions. The 22nd issue of February 1986 announced the organisation of a 'regional G.R.E.C.E. seminar', entitled '*Crise ou guerre économique*',[110] and involving the participation of Bernard Notin, Charles Bressoles, Frédéric Julien and, of course, Guillaume Faye himself. In Italy, the publication of *Contre l'économisme* and *La nouvelle société de consommation* allowed Faye to gain a collaborator within the *Dott.* Marco Tarchi and Mario Bozzi Sentieri would interview Faye on the NR's economic ideas, an interview which, although unpublished in French, would then appear in *Diorama Letterario* (issue number 90, February 1986).

---

107 TN: Orientation/Immigration: Our Position.

108 TN: The Third or the Second Path?

109 TN: Are Women in Control of Their Own Image?

110 TN: Crisis or Economic War?

The Provençal Seminar

In 1984, Faye organised, in collaboration with Tillenon,[111] an S.E.R. seminar that lasted for a week and was held in Provence in the absence of the pontiff, who always created an unwholesome sort of atmosphere through his perpetual complaints and constant whining, which Philippe Baillet would, in two sincerely critical articles published at a much later time, sarcastically label the grumbling of 'Doctor Peutt-Peutt'.[112] In this sweltering month of July 1984, I, too, was there, alongside MC, a friend from Brussels, who had just graduated a week earlier and obtained a doctorate in medicine, thus becoming the youngest doctor in Brussels. I also participated, of course, in the hike across the crests of the Lubéron, setting off from Cucuron, where I took a wonderful photo of Faye, a guitar over his shoulder.

There was yet another major event back then: a seminar on Euro-Arab relations on the premises of the University of Mons in Hainaut, under the guidance of Professor Safar, who taught the Arabic language there. I travelled there myself, as an interpreter for Faye, Bérard and Hadjidinas during their speeches. I was notably responsible for translating a speech given by Karl Höffkes, who, at the time, had ties to Siegfried Bublies' *Wir Selbst* and, being very interested in Gaddafi's social and pan-Africanist ideas, was also in attendance. During this three-day conference, Faye developed a truly colourful relationship with the Vatican representative, Father Michel Lelong, who, in 1975, had been commissioned by Rome to oversee the Islamic-Christian dialogue within the framework of the various initiatives of interreligious dialogues sponsored by the Holy See. Hadjidinas was already ill at the time and, a few days after the conference, had a coffee with me at the Grand Place in Brussels where, in a highly paternal manner, he

---

111 TN: An executive member of G.R.E.C.E. who left the movement at about the same time as Faye.

112 TN: Despite the fact that this invented nickname lacks any proper translation in English, 'Doctor Nag-Nag' would be quite accurate.

expressed his concerns over Guillaume's future. I was very touched by this elderly Greek professor's solicitude, who, on the eve of his death, had sensed the lurking dangers and uncertainty awaiting Faye. Thinking back to it today, I feel a kind of sorrow creeping over me; for we have lost so many good friends!

Faye's situation was becoming increasingly precarious: Jean-Claude Cariou, G.R.E.C.E.'s secretary-general, had been ousted in a particularly vile manner in 1985, only because he had insisted, among many other reasonable demands, on Faye receiving a decent salary and no longer his minimum wage, which he was sometimes given quite reluctantly. All of his theoretical manuscripts, apart from those that were of modest size and suitable for publication in *éléments*, were always rejected. There was only one exception: *Les nouveaux enjeux idéologiques*,[113] published in 'Labyrinthe's' new collection, which would ultimately only comprise two books: Faye's and Carl Schmitt's *Land and Sea*. Cariou's ejection had caused the immediate departure G.R.E.C.E.'s president, the Indianist Jean Varenne, who published a work entitled *Panorama des idées actuelles*,[114] a bibliographical report which Faye reviewed very positively. The departure of the movement's prestigious president robbed Faye of yet another opinion column. Cariou would be replaced by Gilbert Sincyr, who, equally disgusted with the behaviour of some of the pontiff's henchmen and the evil intrigues that they underhandedly weaved on his behalf, would not last long.

Panorama of Current Ideas

Faye's contribution to *Panorama des idées actuelles* (PIA) is also worth mentioning here:

---

113 TN: The New Ideological Stakes.

114 TN: Panorama of Current Ideas.

- PIA number 1 (March 1985): an analysis of Michel Maffesoli's *Essai sur la violence*;[115]

- PIA number 2 (April 1985): an analysis of Gilles Lipovetsky's *L'ère du vide*,[116] in addition to another one by Philippe Baillet (who translated Julius Evola's works) of Faye's *L'Occident comme déclin*;

- PIA number 3 (May 1985): an analysis of Yvan Blot's *Les racines de la liberté*;[117]

- PIA number 4 (June 1985): analyses of Jean Chesneaux's *De la modernité*[118] and Jean Baudrillard's *La gauche divine*;[119]

- PIA number 5/6 (July–August 1985): an analysis of E. R. Dodds' *The Greeks and the Irrational*;

- PIA number 7 (September 1985): an analysis of Stefano Sutti Vaj's *Indagine sui diritti dell'uomo*;[120]

- PIA number 8 (October 1985): analyses of Jürgen Habermas' *Après Marx*[121] and Michel Maffesoli's *La connaissance ordinaire*;[122]

- PIA number 9 (November 1985): analyses of Konrad Lorenz's *Der Abbau des Menschlichen*[123] and Serge-Christophe Kolm's *Le contrat social libéral*;[124]

---

115 TN: Essay on Violence.

116 TN: The Era of Emptiness.

117 TN: The Roots of Freedom.

118 TN: On Modernity.

119 TN: The Divine Left.

120 TN: Investigating Human Rights.

121 TN: After Marx.

122 TN: Ordinary Knowledge.

123 TN: The Waning of Humaneness.

124 TN: The Liberal Social Contract.

- PIA number 10/11 (December 1985/January 1986): an analysis of Martin Heidegger's *Grundbegriffe*;[125]

- PIA number 12 (February 1986): analyses of Carl Schmitt's *Land und Meer*,[126] Lucien Poirier's *Les voies de la stratégie*[127] and Pierre Gallois' *La guerre de cent secondes*;[128]

- PIA number 14 (April 1986): analyses of André Halimi's *Touche pas à l'Amérique*,[129] Jean Baudrillard's *Amérique*[130] and Alain Leroux's *Grands économistes et partis politiques*;[131]

- PIA number 16/17 (June/July 1986): an analysis of Yves Christen's *L'homme bio-culturel*;[132]

- PIA number 18/19 (August/September 1986): analyses of Theodor Adorno's *Prismen*[133] and Alain de Benoist's *Europe, Tiers-Monde, même combat*;[134]

- PIA number 20 (October/November 1986): an analysis of André Brahic's and Pierre Debray-Ritzen's *Conversations dans l'Univers*.[135]

The content of all these PIA-listed works remains, to this day, a set of necessary ingredients that allow one to forge an alternative to the unrealistic and incapacitating mixture of dominant ideologies.

---

125 TN: Basic Concepts.

126 TN: Land and Sea.

127 TN: Strategic Paths.

128 TN: The Hundred Seconds' War.

129 TN: Don't Touch America!

130 TN: America.

131 TN: Great Economists and Political Parties.

132 TN: Bio-Cultural Man.

133 TN: Prisms.

134 TN: Europe and the Third World — the Same Struggle.

135 TN: Conversations in the Universe.

Faye Abandons the 'Madman's Ship'

At the end of 1986, Faye decided to throw in the towel and abandon the 'madman's ship', where there was nothing more that he could do anyway. Even so, he had the courtesy to deliver the speech he had promised to give at the conference held in December 1986, where I myself was called to the rescue: the tone of Faye's speech, which he delivered in the afternoon, did, however, betray his bitterness and discontentment, both of which were fully justified. In 1987, he would write a short text announcing his departure from G.R.E.C.E. and urging his sympathisers to do whatever it took to convey the fundamental message of the metapolitical association; he would distribute the text in Switzerland at the *Lugnasad* rally, on the 1st of August, the Swiss Confederation Day. At a later point, it was I who would translate this text into German for *DESG-Inform*. Faye then participated in the activities of *Ker Vreizh*, the Breton house in the Montparnasse district of Paris headed by Yann-Ber Tillenon and Goulven Pennaod. The friendship between Faye and Tillenon, which began around 1982, had definitely been cemented at that time: it would remain indestructible and serve as proof of exemplary loyalty until Faye's passing in March 2019. This Breton group would then publish the magazine *Diaspad* as part of the 'Maksen Wledig Circle', which is the Celtic name given to the Roman Emperor Maxentius. Faye would entrust this magazine with some of his own texts, which, although surely very relevant indeed, I unfortunately no longer have. An analysis of these articles certainly deserves to be made, so as to pay truly undiminished homage to him and explain each and every stage of his personal and intellectual journey. At the time, this merry bunch of Bretons used to meet at the 'Ti Jos' *crêperie* in the Montparnasse district.

Diaspad and *Kannadig Kêrvreizh Europa*

Faye published many texts in the columns of *Diaspad* and its supplement *Kannadig Kêrvreizh Europa*. The following list is thus non-exhaustive:

- *Faut-il être prosoviétique quand on est anti-occidental?*,[136] Diaspad, issue number 10, 2nd instalment, 1985, pages 8–14;

- *Le traditionalisme… Voilà l'ennemi!*,[137] Kannadig Kêrvreizh Europa, issue number 70–71, pages 3–5 (this article would give rise to heated arguments with the proponents of Evolian and/or Guenonian traditionalism);

- *Infrastructure européenne*,[138] Kannadig Kêrvreizh Europa, issue number 70–71, page 6;

- *Question allemande*,[139] Kannadig Kêrvreizh Europa, issue number 70–71, page 6.

That same year, Faye would publish, with the help of two of his friends, Burgalat and Falavigna, a very original publication entitled *J'ai tout compris*,[140] which would unfortunately only come out on four occasions and include a particularly well-edited issue that centred around AIDS, a major topic at the time, combining humour, cynicism and well-thought-out catastrophism. Krebs would translate into German the issue's most relevant articles devoted to the HIV scourge, the death-sowing virus.

Already in 1985, *Les nouveaux enjeux idéologiques* thus heralded Faye's more controversial works, published by l'Æncre at the beginning of the 2000s, with such chapters as '*Société multiraciale, société*

---

136 TN: Must Anti-Westernists Be Pro-Soviet?

137 TN: Our Enemy? Traditionalism!

138 TN: European Infrastructure.

139 TN: The German Question.

140 TN: Meaning 'I've Understood It All'.

multiraciste,[141] *L'ethnocide des Européens,*[142] *La "tradition" à la lueur de l'âme faustienne*[143] and *L'identité européenne à l'ombre de la technique moderne.*[144]

'Soft' Ideology

Under the pseudonym of Pierre Barbès, Faye would, in cooperation with François-Bernard Huyghe, co-author a very important work in 1987, one which took into account the fact that the 'politically correct' had now become a widespread phenomenon: *La soft-idéologie,*[145] published by Robert Laffont. The book struck me immediately as a fundamental one and so, together with Jean van der Taelen and Guibert de Villenfagne de Sorinnes, we decided to invite Faye and rent a room at the prestigious *Hôtel Métropole,* in the centre of Brussels. Rogelio Pete, who had invited Alain de Benoist as part of a conference on European defence in March 1981, handled the logistics this time around, as he, too, had appreciated the content of *soft idéologie.* The day before the meeting, I received a phone call from a certain G.R.E.C.E. activist who, acting on command, proceeded to shout at me in a most verbose fashion for having launched this initiative. He also targeted Faye with the most despicable insults. I found it easy to tell him that I was not the one organising the event and that he had better address his complaints to Pete, which he obviously could not do, since he did not have our Hispanist friend's phone number. This vociferation, which combined visceral hatred with abysmal stupidity, would have no effect at all, and everything went well. The mighty bigwig had failed to digest Faye and Huyghe's collaboration. In the innermost depths of his

---

141 TN: A Multiracial Society, A Multi-Racist Society.

142 TN: The Ethnocide of European Peoples.

143 TN: 'Tradition' in the Light of the Faustian Soul.

144 TN: European Identity in the Shadow of Modern Technology.

145 TN: Soft Ideology.

stomach, sour secretions of gastric juice generated a ferocious sort of hatred that would never dry up.

Skyrock and *l'Écho des Savanes*[146]

Faye would, however, leave the *Diaspad* orbit so as to initiate his ten-year career at Skyrock, where he would act as 'Skyman' and be involved in all sorts of comedic endeavours, coming up with numerous schoolboy-like sketches, hoaxes and jokes, whose echoes would only reach me indirectly. I vaguely remember a hoax devised by Skyman-the-Avenger, who phoned a rather stupid and flabbergasted lady, telling her that her husband had failed to cover the fees of a famous Lyon-based immunologist, Doctor Belmont. All this in a period of full-fledged AIDS hysteria, of course… One day, the rookie who, in the early 1990s, had been catapulted into the role of G.R.E.C.E.'s 'secretary-general' by the tobacco-addicted Başbuğ[147] called me and, with the bigoted voice of someone who had just been pranked by some rascal and told a salacious story that they were too scandalised to repeat, whispered to me, in an embarrassed tone, that Faye had 'been playing practical jokes' in *l'Écho des Savanes*. Intrigued, I left my office and headed to the neighbourhood newsagent's to purchase the issue, which was fraught with photos revealing those 'practical jokes': Faye had travelled across Paris, disguised as an exasperating man stricken with Down's syndrome,[148] with 'eventful' meals at *l'Hippopotamus*[149] and a walk through the *Saint-Germain-des-Prés* district during which his white blindman's cane struck everything in his path, knocking

---

146 TN: The Savannah Echo.

147 TN: Mehmet İlker Başbuğ was the 26th Chief of the General Staff of Turkey. Initially tried and convicted of having 'founded and led a terrorist organisation', he would be released in 2014, when the Turkish Constitutional Court ruled that his legal rights had been violated, overturning his conviction.

148 TN: The author actually uses the word 'mongoloid'.

149 TN: *Hippopotamus* is a chain of restaurants mainly based in France and specialising in grilled food.

over a postcard display stand and a stack of cans in a *Franprix* super-market. Later on, I would see him again in *Paris Match*, accompanied by his sprightly secretary, Mary Patch (!) — he had become Professor Kervous, one of the personal friends of Bill Clinton, who had just been elected President of the United States. Kervous had been sent on a secret mission to Europe because Clinton had secretly decided to have his own secretary of state for European affairs. The person had to be European, and the first to be given this position would be a Frenchman. Kervous then surveyed a large number of French politicians, who jostled one another in a desire to get the job, maligning their own colleagues. Mary Patch recorded the whole thing, which would then make a great addition to *Paris Match*. Next, we had Faye impersonating a Lithuanian painter, who was presented as a personal friend of the newly elected president of de-Sovietised Lithuania. In the space of twenty-four hours, Faye and his accomplices had painted about twenty canvases representing gloriously erect phalluses, which they would exhibit the following day in a gallery, to be sold at a premium. And it worked! They would reimburse their buyers on the next day, explaining that it had all been a mere hoax, yet the political message, a highly perspicuous one, was crystal clear: all so-called contemporary art is but a great scam — and Faye and his facetious friends had just proved it!

Erik Arckens' Dissertation

A university-related consecration would, however, see the light in 1989, with the publication of Erik Arckens' university dissertation, circulated at KUL (Louvain) under the guidance of two professors: Doctor L. Preneel and E. De Jonghe. This dissertation in political science, which would be awarded the highest possible distinction, undoubtedly constituted, at the time, the best background work on the French NR (*De "nouvelle droite" alsideologietegen de Westerseconsumptiemaatschappij. Eenbenadering*). Arckens was received by the pontiff as if he were a dog that had interrupted a game of skittles. He had asked me to introduce him to the 'Pope', who, in my own presence, welcomed him inside his pigsty of an office, in a display of consummate boorishness, answering his highly relevant questions in an evasive, dry and coarse manner while keeping his stinky cigarette in his mouth and continuing to cut out various newspaper articles, thus earning himself, in the region of Flanders, the nickname '*Ayatollah knip-knip*'. For their part, Pierre Krebs' (female) German friends had picked up a great word from Faye and labelled him *Der Komkomber* (the 'Cucumber'). In his dissertation, Arckens had perfectly perceived Faye's crucial contribution to the development, and especially the ripening, of the neo-rightist ideology. In a chapter entitled '*Les séismographes de la modernité*',[150] Arckens dissected the relevant manner in which Faye had brought essential references to the table, including Veblen, Lasch, Lipovetsky and Baudrillard. Through the filter of Faye's readings, the NR had acquired a new dimension, a non-backward-looking and non-nostalgic one that bestowed upon it its own originality. In his fourth chapter, our Flemish political scientist carried out an in-depth analysis of Faye's notion of system and contrasted it with that of the Frankfurt School. It goes without saying that the pontiff's thurifers never mentioned this outstanding publication, nor did they, of course, ever interview its author or thank him, just as the pontiff never deigned to greet the Dutch translator of his own works during the conferences organised by his deputy. The unfortunate sinologist Alfred Vierling would never manage to stomach the Parisian oaf's colossal loutishness. In the homage that he would pay Faye as part of the latter's obituary, he would recall the situation most opportunely, stating that Guillaume had shown great amiability in comforting him and enlightening him as to the pontiff's true nature.

In 1995, my Italian friends at 'Edizioni Barbarossa', which published its own 'Sinergieeuropee' collection, asked me, with the persistent

---

150 TN: The Seismographs of Modernity.

support of Stefano Vaj, to write a preface to the new Italian edition of *Système à tuer les peuples*. I thus seized the opportunity to offer an in-depth explanation of the philosophical content characterising Faye's approaches[151] and to denounce the mechanisms that had led to his ejection from a movement to which he had, so very generously and without the slightest hesitation, devoted all of his youth, abandoning his uncompleted studies so as to serve a pontiff who would never cease to put a spoke in his wheel.

The Great Return

Then, suddenly, at the end of 1997, an interview with Faye appeared in a new magazine that would gain ground: *Réfléchir et Agir*,[152] run at the time by Eric Rossi. This interview had been obtained by 'DW', an activist of the movement, who, unfortunately for him, had been drawn into a scandalous and ridiculous scam devised by a phoney architect and a dental technician, who were supposedly 'friends of the community'. One of them was, for a time, the main coordinator at the URPIF ('Unité Régionale de Paris-Île-de-France'[153]) and the other one of the pontiff's faithful supporters (and remained so for a long time); he also acted, on occasion, as the group's[154] vocalist but, alas, the poor fellow is afflicted with a voice reminiscent of a damaged rattle, which earned him the nickname 'Cacofonix'.[155] The worst part is that he does not realise this and takes himself for a 'great artist', bulging his worthless

---

151 AN: http://robertsteuckers.blogspot.com/2012/01/lapport-de-guillaume-faye-la-nouvelle.html.

152 TN: Thinking and Acting.

153 TN: The Paris-Île-de-France Regional Unit.

154 TN: It is unclear what 'group' the author is referring to. I can only assume that it is somehow connected to the scam mentioned a few lines earlier, though I am quite unsure.

155 TN: Cacofonix is the English name given to the village bard in the Asterix series. As one can infer from his name, his singing/playing is anything but pleasant.

carina at will. This situation has allowed many a comedian to sneer or laugh. This pathetic 'bard' did, however, have the merit of helping Faye financially and logistically when the latter found himself broke after his departure from G.R.E.C.E. and of paying off some of the debts run up by our friend, who had organised an avant-garde day known as '*Avant-Guerre*', which had not been as successful as one would have expected (he thus had his own 'good works', just like the patronesses of the beautiful districts sketched by Aragon…). We must do the little guitar scraper justice; otherwise, the poor bloke will continue to cry his eyes out. DW, who had been manipulated by those two interesting characters, had been compelled to spend six months in a famous hotel in Fleury-Mérogis. Needless to say, this plunged him into a brooding sort of bitterness. He came to join me in Brussels and, over the next months, made me meet with Rossi in Paris (as the latter's university thesis on the national-revolutionary movement was certainly the best we had experienced up to that point), and with a likeable Iraqi philosopher, who, although a Baathist, was also a Marx specialist. Then, one day, DW, that wonderful chap, called me to tell me that, following his interview with *R&A*, Faye had decided to return to 'metapolitics' and that I was the first person he wanted to see again!

And one fine day, in the spring of 1998, Faye arrived in my neighbourhood in Brussels, guided by DW. It had already been eleven years since we last saw each other at the *soft-ideology* conference in the Metropolis and the Lugnasad rally organised by Pascal Junod on 1st August, 1987 in the Vaud district. But we immediately got talking as if there had been no hiatus, as if the last S.E.R. meeting had only taken place a week earlier. We withdrew to have lunch at the '*Cent Histoires*'[156] café, run by the famous Hubert, a native of Bütgenbach, a municipality in the German-speaking cantons of Belgium. By a happy coincidence, Faye had arrived in Brussels when some of my German friends were also staying there, as was Tomislav Sunic. They all approached him

---

156 TN: One Hundred Stories.

with questions and rekindled past memories, while others, unaware of anything, were delighted to chat with Skyman, with the author of other funny/dirty jokes or with the colleague of the famous Tabatha Cash, the scandalous host of Skyrock — all of which were things I had never heard of. Wine flowed freely on that day. The bill was getting bigger and Hubert de Bütgenbach's eyes twinkled like Scrooge's at the sight of dollars. In the midst of our libations, we decided that Faye would participate in the 'European Synergies' party conference, which was to be held in Trentino in July. He was to present his new work there, published by l'Æncre : *L'Archéofuturisme*.[157] The book began with a very courteous criticism of the New Right's excesses (its historical and hysterical channel), lines which attest to Faye's affable character, as he was always quick to reconcile with, and forgive, those who had hurt him so very deeply. To formulate this courteous criticism, Faye had prepared a short caustic essay, which, sent to me through DW a few weeks earlier, was entitled '*La ND ou la planète des clowns*'[158] (Come to think of it, this text is still somewhere in my drawers…). He then formulated his main idea of 'Archeofuturism' as a 'response to the catastrophe of modernity' and as an 'alternative to traditionalism'. Following this double introduction centred around the NR's avatars and the definition of 'Archeofuturism', what Faye offered us in his new book was a swarm of various articles, including some relevant pages on the thoughts of Carl Schmitt. Next came two essays: '*Pour une économie mondiale à deux vitesses*'[159] and '*La question ethnique et la question européenne envisagées d'un point de vue archéofuturiste*'.[160] The work ended with a piece of fiction: '*Une journée de Dimitri*

---

157 TN: Published in English by Arktos Media Ltd. in 2010.

158 TN: The NR, the Planet of Clowns.

159 TN: For a Two-Tier Global Economy.

160 TN: The Ethnic Question and the European Question Considered from an Archeofuturistic Perspective.

Leonidovitch Oblomov — Chroniques des temps archéofuturistes.[161] In short, the wheels had, once again, been set in motion.

The Memories of Bertrand de Jouvenel

Charles Champetier, who was, at the time, the lugubrious pontiff's main *factotum*, thus hastened to conduct an interview with Faye for *Élements* magazine. Then came the party conference. We both travelled to Milan by night train, accompanied by Fleur, who worked for l'Æncre editions back then. Loyal to the initial S.E.R. mindset, Stefano Vaj welcomed us most warmly into his very posh club of well-dressed public figures, as if we were lords (when, in actual fact, we were still in our 'battledress', i.e. in our crumpled clothes, and were soaked with sweat after spending an almost sleepless night in those hot cars…). Then we hit the road again, heading towards Trentino, where, having arrived in the evening, we settled in. The next morning, the seminars began and were to include a lecture by Laurent Schang on the work of Bertrand de Jouvenel. He would give it in French in front of a Franco-German group that included the ecologist Baldur Springmann, an 87-year-old pioneer in organic farming who had driven his own car from Hamburg to join us. And it was I who translated Schang's words. As for Faye, he was late coming down from his room. He took his place at the table, listened to this somewhat dull round of speeches and translations for five minutes and then declared: '*I had Jouvenel as a teacher at the end of the 1960s, and this is what he said…*' What followed was a spontaneous and unprepared lecture on the work of Bertrand de Jouvenel. This devil of a Faye still remembered the very essence of Jouvenel's theories on the issue of power, thirty-one years after hearing them at the Sorbonne! What a *tour de force*!

In 2000, following a complaint brought by the usual 'vigilant' individuals against Guillaume's work entitled *La Colonisation de*

---

161 TN: A Day in the Life of Dimitri Leonidovich Oblomov — Chronicles of an Archeofuturistic Era.

l'Europe,[162] the pontiff, scared out of his wits and hoping to clear himself (of what, I wonder?), hatched a plot against Faye, who had returned to the NR's fold less than two years earlier. He proceeded to exclude him from all the bodies that he sponsored and banned his flock from spending time with him and publishing his works. Faye had thus suffered another terrible blow, one from which he would never recover and that would instil unabating despair into the very depths of his heart; the kind of despair that would account for several of his behavioural excesses, which I, for one, never experienced, I hasten to say. Worse still: Alexandre Del Valle, who, at the time, was very much friends with Faye and another victim of the obsessive and vicious retribution exacted by the pontiff's henchmen, had just come across an interview conducted by the editorial staff of the Italian newspaper *Lo Stato* with the two accomplices of the NR's holy of holies (the historical-hysterical channel), i.e. his gloomy lordship de Benoist and his poor servile hired hand, Champetier. In their answers, the two fanciful men proceeded to attack Faye, labelling him a hothead and a 'racist', thus adding, in a most treacherous fashion, grist to his opponents' mill before the *XVIIème Chambre de Paris* tribunal.[163] Del Valle and Faye, both in a state of raging fury, phoned me in Brussels straightaway to inform me of the vile statements published in *Lo Stato*. I thus rummaged through my archives and did indeed find a photocopy of the interview, which my Italian correspondents had recently sent me but which I had not yet had time to read. I immediately translated the replies given by those two wretches and commented them in a rather acerbic manner. Mischievously and spontaneously, I then shared them online to create a bit of a weekly buzz — now that's always fun! To cut to the chase, Champetier reacted immediately and

---

162 TN: *The Colonisation of Europe*, which was published by Arktos Media Ltd. in 2016 and that I had the pleasure of translating.

163 TN: The *XVIIème Chambre de Paris*, literally the '17th Chamber of Paris', is a court that specialises in press-related affairs and falls under the *tribunal de grande instance* (High Court) in Paris.

sent his response to the entire NR database, but forgot to hide the two thousand recipient addresses! I checked them and, to my amazement, found that the addresses of all the journalists working for *Le Monde* and *Le Nouvel Observateur* and those of some ever-watchful associations were being added to the list of sympathisers. In short, this was an act of sheer denunciation and gratuitous wickedness, a deliberate desire to harm. To defend Faye, however, I suddenly — and unexpectedly — had all of the NR's addresses, both new and old, at my disposal. A controversy ensued, exacerbated by a team that had baptised itself 'Cercle Gibelin'[164] and wanted to relocate the temple to the centre of the *urbs* by uniting the vital and now dispersed forces of neo-rightist 'dextrism' and, at last, rid it of the presence of traitors, cowards and modernisers. Right after this controversy, Charles Champetier, who had participated in the stampede against Faye and devoted fourteen years of his young existence to serving the pontiff, from the age of eighteen to the age of thirty-two, was thrown out of the association as if he were the scum of the earth, because his salary was to be given to an old bigwig, who had done so many messed-up things at work that he had been laid off, ending up broke on the pavements of Paris. We would never see our dear old Champetier again. After a few very painful years, during which he is said to have bitterly dwelt on his ejection and dealt with the streak of family setbacks that ensued for his wife and their four poor kids, the unfortunate Charles allegedly landed back on his feet and now focuses on practical ecology issues in the green and joyful countryside, deep within peripheral France, far away from the gases of Paris and the acrid smoke of the cigarettes smoked by his ex-mentor, the emblematic epitome of ingratitude.

---

164 TN: The Ghibelline Circle.

Second Ejection and the 'Beat Generation'

Following his second ejection and the denunciation he had been subjected to, Faye, no doubt deeply hurt and outraged by this wanton betrayal, still managed to maintain his momentum thanks to the unconditional support offered by his editor. The fight had to continue, and one had to make do with what one had to hand, beyond the profound sorrows that one may have felt. In 2000, he participated in the 'European Synergies' conferences held in Gropello di Gavirate, near Varese in Lombardy, and, in 2001, in Vlotho in the Weser Mountains in Lower Saxony. In this idyllic region of the Germanic heart of our Europe, especially during this beautiful summer of 2001, Faye surprised us once again. A young friend, Thierry de Damprichard, gave a talk on the American Beat Generation. In the ensuing debate, which, because of the sweltering afternoon heat, took place between 9 p.m. and 10 p.m., an enthusiastic Faye initiated a refresher course on these American authors, who had been very popular at the time of his youth. Suddenly, he fainted and collapsed, his body all stiff. Our German friends immediately called an ambulance and an emergency physician. Soon, a hospital on wheels stopped in front of the door. Faye was revived by a Swiss friend, who had worked as a rescuer in the Swiss army. However, Faye refused to receive medical treatment. It was a habit of his, which Yann-Ber Tillenon would, in fact, deplore in the beautiful tribute he paid to him, a poignant video that would be shared on YouTube after Faye's passing. The latter then drank a bit, re-joined his young listeners and, without losing his train of thought, finished his lecture on American literature!

In December 2001, we met in Saint-Germain, Paris, for a conference on the euro, which was to be introduced in both France and Belgium a week later. In 2001, Faye would re-write and complete his *Petit Lexique du partisan européen*, published in 1985 by Eurograf in the suburbs of Liège thanks to the people skills exhibited by Jean-Marie Simar, who had not hesitated a second to come to his aid. But for this initiative, this lexicon would have ended up in a waste bin in the offices of *rue Charles-Lecocq*. Expanding and developing it, Faye completely re-worked it in 2001, and from the very first subtitle of this version published by l'Æncre, proceeded to show his hand: *Faire bloc avec des idées claires contre l'ennemi commun*.[165] This 'Manifesto of the European Resistance'[166] would achieve well-deserved success, especially in its German and English versions.

In 2002, l'Æncre would release Faye's *Avant-Guerre — Chronique d'un cataclysme annoncé*,[167] a massive book of three hundred and eighty-two pages with gems that include chapters on 'Operetta Rebels', 'Intellectualism as an Anaesthetic', 'The Political Class as a Gathering of Clowns', the decline of Christianity and its distorted anthropology, and the necessary re-embracement of a 'vitalist philosophy' to fight against 'degenerate thinking'. The year of 2004 would see l'Æncre publish a new book by Faye, *Le coup d'État mondial — Essai sur le nouvel impérialisme américain*.[168] This book is a shrewd analysis of the motivations of American imperialism and proposes, in its eleventh and last chapter, a Euro-Russian-American alliance that Faye terms 'Septentrion'. Our author also targets what he calls AAOH, i.e. 'obsessive and hysterical anti-Americanism'. He calls for realistic criticism and condemns all imprecations disseminated and spread by the anti-imperialistic and anti-American discourse of leftist fringe groups and the sour-tempered pontiff, who had, on two separate occasions, proceeded to drive him out of his movement, the very same movement which Faye regarded, both sadly and bitterly, as being his own 'house' and on whose door he had come to knock as a hopeful twenty-year-old.

---

165 TN: Standing Together, with Clear Ideas, Against the Common Enemy.

166 TN: This, of course, is a reference to — and the subheading of — Faye's early and very influential work, *Why We Fight*.

167 *Prelude to War* (2021).

168 TN: *A Global Coup*, published by Arktos Media Ltd. in 2017: https://en.metapedia.org/wiki/A_Global_Coup.

Regarding my own publications back then, few things would ultimately be released, with the exception of:

- The announcement of Faye's return in the 3rd issue of *Réfléchir & Agir*, with a brief review of his remarks collected by Maxime Lion (in: *Nouvelles de Synergies Européennes*,[169] issue number 30/31, October–December 1997, page 35);

- An interview which Faye granted the *Il giornale d'Italia* daily within the framework of the 1998 'European Synergies' conference: conducted by Michele Fasolo on 24th July, 1998 (in: *Nouvelles de Synergies Européennes*, issue number 35-36, July–September 1998, pages 34–35);

- A statement of Guillaume Faye's positions on the Kosovo war ('*Les gouvernements européens marionnettes des États-Unis*'),[170] an article that had previously been published in Italian in *La Padania*, Lega Nord's daily newspaper, on the 18th and 19th of April 1999 (ex: *Res Publica Europae/Lettre politique*[171] in '*Synergies Européennes*'/ France, issue number 18, May 1999);

- A 'Guillaume Faye' file in the 46th issue of *Nouvelles de Synergies Européennes* (June–July 2000, pages 9 to 16), which comprised a defence of Faye following his expulsion from the NR's networks/ historical channel, as well as a report on the impact which his most recent works had had in Italy. The texts were entitled: '*Faut-il lyncher Guillaume Faye?*'[172] by the late Pierre Maugué; '*Du dextrisme*'[173] by Patrick Canavan, a text that reiterated the views espoused by the '*Cercle Gibelin*', which intended to set the record straight across the entire neo-rightist movement; '*Questions à la*

---

169 TN: News from the European Synergies.

170 TN: The European Puppet Governments of the United States.

171 TN: *Res Publica Europae*/Political Letter.

172 TN: Should Guillaume Faye Be Lynched?

173 TN: 'Dextrism' (Rightism).

"nouvelle droite" — *La ND française à la croisée des chemins*,[174] also by Pierre Maugué; *'Déracinement ou archéofuturisme?'*[175] by Professor Augusto Zuliani (a review published in the Milanese daily *La Padania* on 24th February, 2000); *Guillaume Faye ou des racines archaïques du futur*[176] by Angelo Mellone, published in the prestigious magazine *Area* in March 2000; and *Archéofuturisme: cette civilisation ne passera pas la nuit*[177] by Claudia Gualdana (an article previously published in the *Il Sole-24 Ore* daily newspaper, on 30th January, 2000);

- An interview with Guillaume Faye in *Au fil de l'épée*,[178] issue number 30, February 2002, conducted by Victor Marck and taken from the net. In it, Faye talks about his new book, *Avant-Guerre*;

- An article in defence of Guillaume Faye, who had been insulted in *Éléments* magazine by a certain Jean-Charles Personne, nick-named 'Private Nemo'. Lothaire Demambourg had dipped his pen in the acid of vitriol to castigate, in the style of Léon Bloy,[179] those who, ever the members of the same clique, had once again dragged Faye through the mud (in *Au fil de l'épée*, 46th collection, June 2003). The resulting controversy was quite something!

Convergence of Catastrophes

Between 2000 and 2007, Faye came to Belgium on several occasions to present his theories and books. In 2004, we both found ourselves in Ghent. Faye would participate in several colloquiums at Château Coloma, in Sint-Pieters-Leeuw, on the initiative of Georges Hupin,

---

174 TN: Questions for the 'New Right' — the French New Right at a Crossroads.

175 TN: Uprooting or Archeofuturism?

176 TN: Guillaume Faye or the Archaic Roots of the Future.

177 TN: Archeofuturism: This civilisation Shall Not Last the Night.

178 TN: The Edge of the Sword.

179 TN: Léon Bloy (11th July, 1846–3rd November, 1917) was a French novelist, essay-ist, pamphleteer and poet.

who, alongside his wife, would always welcome him with paternal kindness in their beautiful home in the 'Art Nouveau' district of Antwerp. In 2006, we would join forces in the Ravensteinhof hall in Brussels to present his *Convergence des catastrophes*,[180] an excellent book, which he had written in 2004 under the pseudonym of Guillaume Corvus.[181] In 2007, we participated in a colloquium in Dendermonde organised by Kris Roman, the head of the 'EuroRus' association, whose aim is to enable a successful overcoming of Westernism in Europe, one that would involve, as a corollary, a final reconciliation with Russia. Kris Roman would also invite Faye to participate in a debate with the Russian thinker Pavel Tulaev, especially with regard to the notion of 'Euro-Siberia', which our Russian friend found inadequate, since Siberia has never constituted a historical subject; indeed, history has only revolved around Russia in this immense region of the world — at least following the disappearance of the great Genghis-Khanic assemblage. The debate was held in a courteous atmosphere in Roman's beautiful library.

Meeting with Jules Dufresne

In 2007, Guillaume Faye met Jules Dufresne, a very young man who had just founded the *Éditions du Lore*. The latter would publish its first book during that very same year, a book which would arouse great and long-lasting controversy: *La nouvelle question juive*[182] (2007). It is obviously the topic that has angered people, as the positions adopted by Faye have not satisfied anyone — no point in trying to hide this. Personally, I think that he should not have tackled the subject at all, since the category in which one had already classified him (especially when one considers the lawsuit he had faced following the publication of *La Colonisation de l'Europe*) made it impossible for him to approach

---

180 TN: *Convergence of Catastrophes*, published by Arktos Media Ltd. in 2012.

181 AN: And here is my contribution to this common lecture: http://robertsteuck-ers.blogspot.com/2013/12/guillaume-faye-et-la-convergence-des.html.

182 TN: The New Jewish Question.

the Jewish question in a serene way, even if he did have the praiseworthy intention of putting an end to monomaniacal concerns that were
often sterile and expressed in the various cenacles where one typically
encountered them (i.e. national pro-Palestinian ones; national philo-
Zionist ones; pro-Palestinian ones, either in favour or opposed to immigration; anti-Zionist ones condemning immigration, etc.). Despite
the three hundred and ninety-six pages that he filled with extensive
thoughts when trying to deal with all of the issue's facets, he failed to
create a new consensus on this thorny problem. He, instead, earned
himself a 'Zionist' label and the nickname 'Shabbat-goy', which he
shared with Del Valle.[183] The book, however, remains symptomatic of
a state of mind that actually reigned in non-conformist circles during
the first decade of the 21st century. Reading it is therefore essential; for
informational purposes.

Wofür wir kämpfen[184]

Pierre Krebs, who we met for the first time in 1981 in the apartment
of the young woman that was accommodating Faye in her maid's
room and that had, incidentally, served the sinister pontiff his *rillettes*
between Hong Kong and Las Vegas, published a German version of
Pourquoi nous combattons (Wofür wir kämpfen) in 2006. He prefaced
it with Andreas Molau, who immediately invited Faye to Bayreuth, at
the end of April, for a prestigious German-European conference, during which Enrique Ravello and I also took the floor. At the last moment, the pontiff's emissaries tried to sabotage the publication of this
edition, which had been announced during the conference: visibly
upset, Faye noticed their little game and spoke to me about it, because

---

183 TN: Born Marc d'Anna on 4th September, 1968, Alexandre del Valle is a French
     author, professor, columnist, and political commentator. He is particularly
     famous for his analysis of Islamic extremism, as well as his criticism of the
     neo-Ottoman, Islamist and post-Kemalist Turkey established by Recep Tayyip
     Erdoğan. Del Valle is an advocate of the so-called 'PanWest paradigm, i.e. of a
     cooperation between the West and Russia in the face of radical Islamism.

184 TN: Literally (and correctly) 'What We Fight For', otherwise 'Why We Fight'.

this attempt had, once again, twisted the knife in the secret wound he bore, which, however invisible, remained a festering one... I immediately rushed towards the two idiots, who were good men at heart but slightly disabled brain-wise, and told them: 'Fantastic news! A book by Guillaume Faye will finally be published in German! We must rejoice! He's such a great man! And to think that envious people have always denigrated this outstanding orator!' They did not dare to contradict me. The usual pesterers had thus, once again, proceeded to flog a dead horse. Another miss, *caramba*! Krebs and Molau had refused to yield. That's what I like about this environment: *Beharrungsmenschen*![185]

One would have to wait until 2011 for *éditions du Lore*, which was still run by Jules Dufresne, to publish *Sexe et dévoiement*, an effort spanning across three hundred and seventy-one pages that recapitulate all of Faye's ideas on sexuality and the history of sexuality, from antiquity to Christianisation and from the modern era to the postmodern one — an unequalled feat in the movement. The book acts as an expanded and comprehensive version of the brochure he penned in 1983, namely *Sexe et idéologie*. In 2012, *éditions du Lore* would release two new works written by Faye — *Mon programme*[186] and *Archéofuturisme V2.0*.[187] As suggested by its title, *Mon programme* comprises a political programme that must be implemented immediately should there suddenly be a power vacuum, which only we are able to fill. The text can still serve as a source of inspiration, but let us not forget that our political reality is becoming increasingly volatile, and this type of programme is thus quickly rendered obsolete. As for *Archéofuturisme V2.0*, it centres around a series of 'cataclysmic stories', which have the great merit of being original while also revealing a novelistic facet of Faye's that he would not make much use of in the end. In early 2013, *Lore* would publish a brochure in the style of those that were once produced by G.R.E.C.E. Its title? *La nouvelle lutte des*

---

185 TN: Persistent people.

186 TN: My Programme.

187 TN: *Archeofuturism 2.0*, published by Arktos Media Ltd. in 2016.

classes.[188] In it, Faye announces a social collapse, one that shall be due, among other reasons, to an exponential increase of parasitic casts that are uselessly imported and do not contribute in any way to the wealth of the nation. This brochure is thus part of the logic inaugurated in *La Colonisation de l'Europe*. Its publication marked the end of Faye's cooperation with *éditions du Lore*.

Faye would subsequently cooperate with *Tatamis* editions, headed by Jean Robin. This publishing house would then release his *Comprendre l'islam*, of which I do not (yet) have a copy. Finally, Faye would turn to a fifth publisher, Daniel Conversano, to release his last book, *La guerre civile raciale*,[189] which I look forward to having.

Breaking Through the Anglosphere

Faye's major breakthrough, however, came in the Anglo-Saxon countries during the second decade of the twenty-first century. Thanks to Arktos editions, sponsored by the Swede Daniel Friberg and the American John Morgan,[190] Faye's books would enjoy much greater print runs than in France and a global marketing that owes a lot to the excellent and properly annotated translations. Here is the list:

- *Archeofuturism* (2010);

- *Why We Fight* (2011);

- *Convergence of Catastrophes* (2012);

- *Sex and Deviance* (2014);

- *The Colonisation of Europe* (2016);

---

188 TN: The New Class Struggle.

189 TN: *A Racial Civil War*, which Arktos Media Ltd. was compelled to publish as *Ethnic Apocalypse* (2019) so as to avoid shocking all those politically correct censors out there.

190 TN: John Morgan's involvement is, of course, no longer actual, as he and Arktos Media Ltd. parted ways several years ago.

- *Archeofuturism 2.0* (2016);

- *Understanding Islam* (2016);

- *A Global Coup* (2017).

Within the vast American movement, no attempt to sabotage his books has ever taken place. They are continuously advertised through Greg Johnson and Jared Taylor's websites, which have been emulated in this regard by many others. The social network hype surrounding Faye's works has thus been constant there. The American specialist on the French 'New Right', the formidable Michael O'Meara, has devoted a short book to him entitled *Guillaume Faye and the Battle of Europe* (Arktos, 2013), which has the merit of explaining Faye's work by supporting each argument with solid and extensive notes. In the only American copy of his work that I actually have, namely *Why we Fight*, which Faye gave me in Paris on 4th June, 2011, I discovered a preface written by O'Meara in which Faye is described as the prophet of the 'Fourth Age', followed by an English translation of the German preface by Krebs. The names of all those who contributed to this English edition of *Why We Fight* appear on page 4: the translator, O'Meara; the editor, John Morgan; the Australian co-editor and expert in the French language, Matthew Peters; the cover designer, Andreas Nilsson; and the unmissable Daniel Friberg. It would seem that this excellent team was not pestered by the louses that the guru usually sent from his dark Parisian backroom… Very recently, a few days before Faye's final passing, the guru spewed out his anger and spite (hardy-har-har!) in the columns of the Italian daily *La Reppublica*: the representatives of the Alt-Right current are nothing but 'ridiculous little extremists', he proclaimed, indifferent to the fact that they just so happen to have actually financed the fine editions of his own works, not to mention a few pleasure trips to the Americas… Always this deep-seated ingratitude characterising the irremovable 'Doctor Peutt-Peutt'…

When Clearing One's Name Is Fruitless

Pontiff Peutt-Peutt's efforts to clear his own name have had no impact whatsoever and have remained absolutely useless: on 28th March, 2019, twenty-two days after Faye's passing, an extensive 'study' by a certain Dan Glazebrook appeared on the 'Democracy and Class Struggle' website.[191] It is a long, soft-brained, and antifa-like text about the big manitou with whom Faye and I rubbed shoulders for so long. Let us judge for ourselves: the Manitou is the man who has 'browned the Left' — *'But perhaps the most important figure in the fascist appropriation of leftist concepts in the service of a more "politically-correct" fascism is Alain de Benoist'*; *'Benoist's political career began as straightforward cheerleading for jingoistic imperialism in books like "Courage Is their Homeland" and "Rhodesia — Land of the Faithful lions'*; *'Benoist drew on the concepts of the New Left to fashion an explicitly fascist form of identity politics'*; *'His "Nouvelle Droite" movement directly lifted New Left catchphrases about "respect for diversity" and the "right to difference" to advocate a politics of racially-purified ethnic separation'*; *'This was essentially a rehashing of the global apartheid theories of the nineteenth century racists, who Benoist explicitly sought to rehabilitate'*; *'In this way, notes Reid-Ross, Benoist sought to implement Hitler's injunction to create a people who are "ready" for fascism'*; *'In other words, Benoist effectively lay the groundwork for the white "identity politics" at the heart of modern fascism'*. All of this, I agree, is the abstruse blabbing that we have been hearing for many decades and which serves as an indication of severe mental petrification; but, lo and behold, these accusations will no longer be, in the near future, aimed at Faye, the man who did not mince his words, but, instead, at the one who always systematically strived to sink him in the hope of clearing himself, of being accepted by the system's fogeys as a gentle intellectual moderate, who stood up to the evil Faye, i.e. to the nasty pit bull, who

---

191 AN: Democracy and Class Struggle — *'The Browning of the Left: How Fascists Colonised Anti-Imperialism'*: https://democracyandclasstruggle. blogspot.com/2019/03/.

wanted to bite those poor Salafists and the postmodern Savonarola,[192] who never stopped slandering those nice Wahhabis (all of this with the alleged and highly hypothetical help of the Tsahal), and opposed the American Alt-Right, made up of 'ridiculous little extremists', who exploit his august person to assert themselves (as if, to raise their own status, those people actually needed an old Parisian driveller who has acted as the interlocutor of further senile drivellers on the other side of the spectrum, in the columns of *Le Figaro* or *Causeur*…). Faye expressed himself most accurately when talking about the 'redeemed ones', and, conversely, this Dan Glazebrook person has confirmed it all. Let us now heed Faye's words: '[…] *those who, in the past, have gone off course, committed sins of youth and dreadfully strayed from the straight and narrow, and who long to be forgiven by redeeming themselves. Alas, they fail to free themselves from the tinkling pans attached to their tails, no matter their effort and agitation and no matter how much they crawl, lick themselves clean or return favours.*' (*Avant-guerre*, page 207). QED.

In October 2018, several friends called me to tell me that Guillaume Faye's state of health was alarming and that he had been hospitalised. And we all know the rest. And yet, his response to the doctors and friends, who did not attempt to hide the truth from him, was truly amazing, and I am certain we would all like to display the same cold serenity during our last moments: 'I am sixty-nine years old, and I shall die at the same age as Plato — of cancer, just as he did'. Atropos cut the last thread that still linked him to life on 6th March, 2019, shortly before midnight. His coffin was placed in the family vault, in the cemetery of a village near Poitiers (Faye considered himself to be descended from there). Yann-Ber Tillenon put *Maksen Wledig*'s eagle on his chest. Bruno, a friend, slipped in a map of 'Greater Europe'

---

192 TN: Girolamo Savonarola (21st September, 1452–23rd May, 1498) was an Italian Dominican friar from Ferrara and a preacher in Renaissance Florence. He openly defied and disobeyed the Pope (just as Faye is said to have disobeyed his own 'pope') on several occasions, which led to his excommunication.

(including Siberia), in addition to a poignant text. Philippe Gibelin presided over the ceremony, and Daniel Conversano was among those present. Other friends from the area had also taken the trouble to attend. Floral bouquets surrounded his unfortunate remains, bouquets whose great beauty was due to their great simplicity. I am glad that Faye has been reunited with his land, his family, and his child at the end of his endless wandering in solitude and his continual removal, which was always stamped with the seal of tragedy in spite of his apparent joy, a displayed joy which, in fact, concealed his great pain.

Pierre Vial's Appropriate Words

It was Pierre Vial who came up with the right words to describe Faye's fate. Vial put his finger on the naked, cruel truth that was there to be seen, deep within Faye's own person, and which the latter hid (oh so sadly) behind his colourful panache. With regard to G.R.E.C.E., Vial thus writes:

> His talent has done wonders; maybe too much for certain overinflated egos that he (unintentionally) overshadowed.

I can personally testify to this sentence's relevance and accuracy... Vial goes on to add:

> Once the divorce with certain hierarchs of the New Right had become inevitable, it impacted the very depths of his being, though only few of us ever realised it.

Finally, he states the following:

> There were wounds in him that never fully healed.

These wounds were being constantly reopened by the same despicable individuals because, it must be said, Guillaume was a man one deliberately desired to kill slowly, a man who was literally *kapotgekoeioneerd* or *kaputtkujoniert*, as we say in Dutch and German (meaning that he was 'taken for a fool' and cheated, to extrapolate from Vial's words a little); a desire and will that did not emanate from the enemy camp but his own! This was achieved by humiliating him and insulting him all day long in the 1980s, at a time when his work was exemplary, and spreading the worst possible gossip about him in the 1990s and 2000s. And yet there are none here, in the former Austrian Netherlands, or in the United States, who have ever witnessed or, a fortiori, been subjected to the behaviour one attributed to him, except perhaps his third publisher, Jules Dufresne, in Brittany (yet this is undoubtedly the case because of the mead that he so generously serves his guests and authors...). None of those who regularly accommodated him, whether Georges Hupin, Guibert de Villenfagne, Kris Roman, Jared Taylor or myself, ever had anything to complain about. Neither did those who offered us accommodation during the various party conferences held in Italy or Germany. I therefore say: shame on all those who, in the past, hurt him without reason, in a display of abject and disturbing cruelty (from a mental health perspective), and those who continually vilified him! And most of all, shame on 'those who knew him' and still insulted him, even a few days before he was entombed in the ground, thus deserving to be labelled a 'clique', a label which one of our old comrades, and not a meaningless one by any means, stamped them with in a letter addressed to me personally. Shame, furthermore, on those insignificant and brainless curmudgeons who obsequiously serve the hateful elders of the 'clique' and gleefully spread their spiteful sentences across the great web.[193]

Tillenon: 'Faye Is a Multifaceted Man'

If Vial, using a few perfectly crafted sentences, managed to put his finger on the very profundity of the psychological problem that had burdened Faye's person, on this unspeakable, immense and incurable sadness that had slowly transformed him and condemned the generous, happy and curious boy he was to becoming a man who, for

---

193 TN: Meaning the Internet.

ten whole years, had fallen prey to a farce, which he longed to free himself of, a man who had aged prematurely and been undermined by a most insidious evil, it was Yann-Ber Tillenon who, in a first video, succeeded in paying just tribute to Faye for displaying multiple facets. Tillenon perceives Faye as a thinker, a polemicist, a hoax screenwriter, a comic book author, and an actor capable of playing any role — a statement which Faye himself corroborated in a recent programme aired on 'TV Libertés', when he stated that he had always sought to achieve such multi-dimensionality, one that was also representative of the Greek philosophers of antiquity, his role models. Indeed, Faye's line of thought is a response to the one-dimensionality of the bourgeois world, which had, at the beginning, been his own and which he had then rejected with every fibre of his being to devote himself entirely to the cause, all to the detriment of his family life and of any consistent professional career. His response to one-dimensionality (that of the Demesmaeker type) was obviously not identical to the one proposed by Herbert Marcuse, even if Faye did want a return to the Greeks, particularly to Aristotle (a fact which brought him closer to Ivan Blot, who passed away in October 2018) and Heraclitus, and rejected what he, alongside Raymond Ruyer (1902–1987), termed 'ideological nuisances'; all of which stem from misguided modernity.

Faye had got to know G.R.E.C.E. at a time when the latter had its own socio-political circle in Paris (the 'Pareto Circle') and when, in harmony with the lessons learnt from the German sociologist Henning Eichberg at the 'Domus', in the Aix region, the movement's leaders dedicated their efforts to the logical empiricism of the English school and Ludwig Wittgenstein's *Tractatus Logico-Philosophicus*[194] — a domain which, at the time, also interested Raymond Ruyer, who taught in Nancy and was a member of *Nouvelle école*'s patronage committee. In the eyes of the English empiricist school/English logic, as well as those of Ruyer, Wittgenstein's disciples and their German

---

194 TN: Latin for 'Logical Philosophical Treatise' or 'Treatise on Logic and Philosophy'.

national-revolutionary interpreter Eichberg, scientific and political discourse had to be crystal clear, logical, and devoid of any and all ambiguities and incapacitating affect.[195] Having read Heidegger's works and his *Letter on Humanism*,[196] Faye understood perfectly well that such pure scholastic logic did not suit the ever-turbulent sphere of politics, which is always greatly impacted by irrationality, whether destructively or constructively. He did, however, display a clear will to incontrovertibly reject all ambiguities, incapacitating affective states and sterilising refrains, all of which generated immobilisations that had to be smashed with a Nietzschean hammer (as was the case when he impersonated a fashionable 'Lithuanian painter'...). Faye said he was 'realistic and accepting', in contrast to the craze for pure and de-constructivist criticism, on which intellectual leftists had chosen to bet when riding on the coat-tails of the Frankfurt school, of French deconstructivism (the 'French School') and of other intellectualist lines of thoughts. The fact that these failings were being imitated by the sycophants of our own movement had to be rejected just as vigorously. In order to evade this lack of realism, these 'ideological nuisances' and incapacitating affective states, it was necessary to revive the Hellenic spirit of antiquity in which Faye had basked (and enjoyed basking) as a teenager, in his college in Angoulême. A new Greek *paedia*[197] and an immersion in the Roman *mos maiorum*[198] are the antidotes to the drifts of late modernity.

Our movement was therefore required to avoid taking account of ideological nuisances, whose purpose is to enable one to participate in the sterile debates orchestrated by the media of the people-killing system, debates in which 'one discusses the sex of snails' (see Faye's *Avant-guerre*, page 206). The only thing one had to take into consideration were the facts, thus becoming a 'factualist' in some way, and not the

---

195 TN: In psychology, the term 'affect' refers to emotions or desires that influence one's behaviour.

196 TN: Originally titled *Über den Humanismus*.

197 TN: Theory or teaching method.

198 TN: 'Ancestral custom' or 'way of the ancestors'.

vague ideas that the 'French intellectual landscape' cheerfully toyed with while our entire society simply went down the toilet (*'Contre le byzantinisme, retour au réel!'*,[199] ibid). The pontiff's major mistake was, therefore, that of wanting to take control of platforms where, in fact, nothing specific or 'earth-shattering' was ever said. As for Faeyan paganism, it was classic, Hellenic and Roman, for it thus allowed one to reconnect with classical humanities, without falling into the excesses of the New Age, of those that had misread Tolkien, of hippies that had been recycled through some kind of soft 'folcism',[200] etc. In his text on Faye dated 7th March 2019[201] (the day when we all learnt of our friend's passing), Benedikt Kaiser, the representative of the latest generation of the German *Neue Rechte*, speaks of his desire to become anchored in reality, of his *Wille zur realpolitischen Erdung*[202] — a nice turn of phrase that would not, however, prevent him from loafing around in the pontiff's ass-kisser club, all in the futile hope of receiving a friendly pat on the right cheek… He has already offered all the necessary guarantees in this regard.

Art of the Memory

Thanks to the education he received in a Jesuit college, Faye also practiced, if you ask me, the so-called 'arts of the memory'. He was thus sometimes able to prepare a magnificent two-hour lecture by scribbling the outline on a small piece of crumpled paper, or even a beer mat, using only a few key words and a 'path' comprising no more than a few lines and arrows. His speech on Jouvenel in Trentino, back in July 1998, proved that he retained some of these 'paths' somewhere at the back of his brain and could immediately bring them to mind. It is an art that has now been largely forgotten in Europe.

---

199 TN: Against Byzantinism: Returning to Reality!

200 TN: This seems to be yet another neologism referring to some kind of folkish attitude.

201 AN: https://sezession.de/60561.

202 TN: Literally 'will to Realpolitik-based anchoring'.

I have thus lost the person alongside whom I walked for forty-four long years, even if we had, admittedly, not been colleagues for the past two decades — indeed, our essential standpoints never ceased to unite us intellectually. I could still add a thousand and one things about Faye, but I feel that I have already shared some crucial lines of thought to be followed by those that shall write about the movement's history (a movement to which Guillaume Faye dedicated his best initiatives but which drove him out and denied him), as well as those who wish to understand its motivations while espousing its essential views, beyond the wickedness of certain hierarchs who, for their part, deserve to be forgotten and, at the very least, be prevented from sitting at our dining table. We could indeed do without such dinner companions. What one must, however, bear in mind is that the ideas remain, for they were there before our time and subsist once we are gone; men, by contrast, are temporary, regardless of whether they belong to the best or the worst of us, since they are very often subject to failure.

Whatever the case, there are no words that could enable me to fully express my gratitude to Faye for all that he has given me. So, thank you, Guillaume, may you rest in peace in the Poitou soil, alongside your parents, near *Futuroscope*[203]... Earth and rockets!

ROBERT STEUCKERS,
Forest-Flotzenberg,
March 2019

---

203 TN: *Futuroscope* or *Parc du Futuroscope* is a French theme park that focuses on multimedia-related developments, futuristic advances/aspects, state-of the-art audio-visual technology, holographic entertainment, etc. It comprises several 3D cinemas, some 4D cinemas and other attractions and shows, some of which are globally unique. It even offers people the opportunity to visit a rotating observatory that lifts them to a height of 150 feet.

III

Guillaume Faye, an Awakener of the Twenty-First Century

By Pierre-Émile Blairon

G ood evening, my friends,

Thank you for being here, and thank you, Richard Roudier, for inviting me to recall the memory of one of our dearest friends, a man who left us on the night of 6th–7th March, 2019 — Guillaume Faye. It was on the 13th of March, in a small cemetery in Poitou, on a rainy and gloomy day, when, among people that I had not seen for years, I asked myself the following question:

What Is a Friend?

A friend is someone you do not ask for anything and who does not ask you for anything, either; someone who you do not need and who does not need you; someone who, regardless of whether you see them every day or every three years, is always there, on a permanent basis, and who you know has a life that runs in parallel to yours, having the same reactions as you no matter the subject, even when he is on the other end of the planet. He is your double, and there is thus no need to look at his photo — just look in a mirror instead. You might ask me now: what's the use of having a friend, then? His presence in your life allows you to know you are not alone in the world, even when what you love most in the world is actually your solitude. In our community, however, a friend is more than that. Why? Because we do not participate in the world as it is but reject it, and it is that friend who renders it acceptable for us; and because we are a very small minority of lucid and aware people. In the world we live in, friendship is a *fraternity of differentiated beings*, of men who stand among the ruins, as Evola once said, because they are lucid and aware and thus suffer more than others when seeing their country, whose culture is among those that have offered the world the most, degraded to the level of a banana republic; when watching as a European heritage that dates back thousands of years is abandoned by those that are in charge of preserving it; and when witnessing the sullying of their ancestors' soil at the hands of entire hordes of non-European populations, who do not respect the land that welcomes them.

Westernists

I belong to Richard's generation; to put things in perspective, I was twenty years old in 1968, and we started campaigning in the late 1960s. At the time, most of us lacked well-formed ideas, and as for our references, they dated back to the post-war period or the war of Algeria. We were all either nationalists or regionalists, through atavism and intuition, yet did not have any solid political or doctrinal education, much less an intellectual one — we were what one terms 'activists', or grassroots activists, to be specific. What we mainly had were role models, heroes that stemmed from recent history and included Captain Sergent, the captain of the Legion, who was one of the main leaders of the OAS and founded the *Mouvement Jeune Révolution* (MJR),[1] in which I myself was involved as an activist after my association with *Occident*[2] and before joining *Ordre nouveau*.[3] We were 'Westernists'

---

1   TN: The *Mouvement Jeune Révolution* (Young Revolution Movement) was a French 'extreme-rightist' movement. Although deeply influenced by social Catholicism and the resistance movement initiated by the OAS, the group's discourse actually swerved left after the events of May 1968.

2   TN: *Occident* was an extreme-right militant group and was active in France between the years of 1964 and 1968. It was regarded as the 'main activist group in the extreme-right spectrum during the 1960s'. *Occident* activists were famous for their 'commando' actions aimed at a wide range of 'enemy' targets, which included left-wing students, French Communist Party offices, immigrant associations, and anti-colonialists.

3   TN: *Ordre nouveau* ('New Order') was a nationalist movement created on December 15, 1969. In June 1972, *Ordre nouveau* joined with Jean-Marie Le Pen's movement and became part of Front National.

back then, as expressed by the very name given to the first militant movement to which I belonged, *Occident*, i.e. the nation + Europe + America, and, for some, even Israel.

However, it was only when I learnt to separate Europe from the West — especially thanks to Guillaume — that I became a European regionalist.

We were anti-Marxists, anti-Gaullists, anti-immigrationists, and, in fact, rather anti-everything than pro-anything. For although we were very young, very ignorant and very rebellious, we had already taken notice of certain dysfunctions characterising the era, and I still remember one of *Ordre nouveau*'s slogans: three million immigrants = three million unemployed people. The same slogan could readily be readopted today, with the figures multiplied by five: fifteen million immigrants = fifteen million unemployed people; which would certainly correspond to the actual figures being concealed from us.

Those who, at the time, were involved as activists in these 'nationalistic' groups were at least as opposed to bourgeois society as their leftist enemies, i.e. the petty bourgeois and sons of the great bourgeois that actually launched the rebellion of May 1968. Most of the leaders of the May 1968 movement are now in key positions in the capitalist and uniformist society they had previously denounced. It must, however, be said that, even on our side, very few have retained the convictions they espoused during their youth — indeed, the vast majority of those who once struggled as activists by our side have now fallen into line and melted into the masses. Only a small elite have continued in their militant fight, and awakeners all stem from this small elite.

It was around that very same time, approximately in 1968, that a certain group surfaced, one which was initially known as *Europe-Action* and had been founded by Dominique Venner.[4] The group was,

---

4   TN: Dominique Venner (16th April, 1935–21st May, 2013) was a French historian, journalist and essayist, in addition to being a member of the OAS and the founder of *Europe-Action*. He later embraced white nationalism before

in part, also rooted in the Algerian adventure. And when I say 'adventure', it is, of course, in the noble sense of the word — I should thus use the term 'epic', rather. For it was with them, and thanks to them, that most of us received our first decent political and metapolitical education. And what is most important, in my opinion, is the fact that it was thanks to this group that we encountered our true identity, that of our pre-Christian Gallic past, and discovered our own roots. The foundations had thus been laid, and all that remained was for us to construct the house — an undertaking that would mainly be carried out by the one whose memory we are celebrating today: Guillaume Faye.

When the Devil Emerged from His Box

It is from the ranks of this *Europe-Action* group, which had, in part, stemmed from the FEN (Fédération des étudiants nationalistes)[5] and would soon be known as G.R.E.C.E. (the Research and Studies Group for European Civilisation) and then 'Pour la Culture Européenne',[6] that a dashing and well-dressed young man emerged, or should I say arose, like a devil coming out of his box. Having been discovered by Venner, he proceeded to overturn everything with his passion and talent, even sacrosanct standards that had been etched in stone. It just so happens that I myself studied in Aix and remained there, and the group's summer meeting place was actually a large house, the Domus, located near Aix-en-Provence. It was there that I first met the man who would become the brilliant spokesperson and inventive theorist for what would later be termed the 'New Right'. I remember that, even back then, he was more than just an intellectual; he also had a sense of theatrics and farce and would delight us with improvised comedy playlets that made us laugh. Now, however, more than forty years

---

withdrawing from politics in order to devote himself to his career as a historian. He would eventually commit suicide in the Notre-Dame de Paris cathedral.

5   TN: Federation of Nationalist Students.

6   TN: For European Culture.

later, History has issued its verdict — Guillaume Faye was much more than that.

Guillaume Faye, an Awakener

Guillaume Faye was indeed an awakener. Awakeners are men who come from an immanent, immutable and permanent world, that 'other world' that lies parallel to ours, arriving here to accomplish a mission. These men have no other concern than to pass on their knowledge and energy; and their entire life ends up being devoted to this transmission. Awakeners appear in critical periods of history, when everything has been turned upside down and all values reversed, and when the situation seems desperate. They give their mission priority over their own person, their personal interest and their comfort. Their rule of thumb is the following one: *do what you must, without anticipating success.* The La Rochefoucault[7] family had turned this principle into their motto: '*Do what must be done, come what may*'.

I was fortunate enough to meet our main contemporary French awakeners, some of whom were my friends and still are. I could mention, alongside Guillaume himself, Marc Augier, who I met some time before his passing in Lyon; Jean Mabire; Robert Dun, whose real name is Maurice Martin; Pierre Vial, who I actually meet on a regular basis; as well as Paul-Georges Sansonetti. And you are very fortunate indeed to have an entire family of awakeners in your region, the Roudiers! Which is no trivial matter. I am referring to at least two Roudier generations, all of whom are warriors that fight like lions for our cause.

Guillaume Faye had all the characteristics of an awakener, just like all those that I have just mentioned.

---

7   TN: François VI, Duc de La Rochefoucauld, Prince de Marcillac (15th September, 1613–17th March, 1680) was a prominent French writer who penned both maxims and memoirs.

An awakener is, first and foremost, a transmitter, and can set an example and serve as a role model, or even a mentor, though he is not a guru.

Neither is he an intellectual, as is nowadays understood — for an awakener is never amongst us to waste his time on endless discussions, whose purpose is to determine the sex of angels. An awakener is a realist, even if he may seem mystical. He has a mission that he is perfectly aware of and which he must accomplish, for that is his sole purpose on this earth. Everything else is but incidental contingency. When he speaks or writes, he does not express himself in words that no one actually understands, as is the case with those pseudo-intellectuals who need to resort to some sort of jargon so as to make people believe that they are intelligent or to make it perfectly clear to others that they are part of a closed cenacle, which is both ridiculous and pathetic. An awakener has no use of such gimmicks. He does not seek to distinguish himself by seeking novelty at any cost, since there is never anything new under the sun in any case.

An awakener is, furthermore, not a philosopher, whether of the self-proclaimed kind or not, even if he is very much in love with wisdom, as the word 'philosophy' actually indicates. Sadly, the latter has been subjected to so many avatars that it is no longer taken to mean what it genuinely expresses.

An awakener is, likewise, not a 'rebel'; for rebels are always mere pseudo-rebels and are no more rebellious than the hairlocks that they throw back in a display of affectation. What they are is a bunch of hairdressing-salon rebels, weak-willed people that arouse cheap, shiver-inducing emotions within themselves, but the shivers are primarily concerned with their own material comfort and brand image. An awakener is, therefore, not a rebel by any means — what he is, in fact, is a *revolutionary*.

An awakener is a simple and modest man, one who does not need to showcase himself in any way; for only people who perceive themselves as being in a weak position could ever desire to put themselves in the spotlight. He is entirely devoid of vanity and does not suffer from narcissism or having an oversized ego, since such a state is a genuine disease, a pathological state, which has been clearly defined by medical science and which affects virtually every single individual belonging to the ruling classes. When I speak of the ruling classes, it is not only politicians that I have in mind, but also the media, unions, magistrates, profiteering members of the banking industry, NGOs, advertisers, associations, multinationals, entertainers, etc. An awakener can express himself in different ways, depending on his character or the talents which the deities have bestowed upon him so that he may successfully convey the message he has been entrusted with. Guillaume was, among other things, a provocative awakener.

Guillaume the Provocateur

During his last television broadcast, which was part of an interview with *TV Libertés*, Guillaume Faye was labelled a provocateur, notably by Martial Bild;[8] to which Guillaume replied: '*Of course, the very reason I am here is to provoke; provocation is a word that comes from the Latin 'provocare', meaning to encourage others to respond to you, to think'.* In some way, Faye the awakener wanted to immediately ascertain the result of his own work. As suggested by the very word, an awakener's role is to rouse sleeping men, to throw a large bucket of water in the face of the slumbering. He is also the one who, for instance, prevents those lost in an icy desert, high up in the mountains, from falling asleep, as this would, in such a context, bring about those people's death. And we ourselves are, as we speak, in this very context.

I remember being kicked out of a restaurant with Guillaume, because he had expressed, in a loud and clear fashion, thoughts that were

---

8   TN: Born on 12th November, 1961, Martial Bild is a French journalist and politician and a former member of the Front National's political bureau. He also played a major role in the founding of the Party of France in 2009 and established the web television channel *TV Libertés* in 2014.

not politically correct at all. Having tried to silence him, which had only served to encourage him in his speech, the people seated at the table next to ours asked the bistro owner to make us leave. Convinced that they had every right to do so and feeling they were acting on the basis of universal right-mindedness, they threatened to call the police if the owner failed to comply; which he did, because the bistro wanted to avoid a scandal. And since he had used polite words when asking us to leave, we agreed, just as kindly. To my knowledge, Guillaume never got his face smashed in, although this could have happened to him more than once. And thanks to the fact that I continue to follow his example and practice this type of provocation myself, alongside other friends, I have realised that people are too timid to actually dare to reply, simply wondering who those old fools expressing such odd ideas might be — not to mention the fact that they have no counter-arguments to use. Anti-racist propaganda has wreaked havoc among the French, who have been left lifeless, inarticulate, brainless and dazed.

This is, in fact, one of the issues where I disagree with Guillaume: I am, of course, referring to the notion of a French revolutionary awakening on a nation-wide scale, which he expresses in his latest book, *La Guerre civile raciale*. I believe that the French are too anaesthetised to rebel. Indeed, the revolt of the yellow vests never addresses — or hardly ever — the crucial problem of immigration, simply because it is a taboo subject. There have only been a handful of protests against the Marrakech Migration Pact,[9] and they only lasted for a short time. What I believe instead is that an awakening, if one ever occurs, can

---

9   TN: The Global Compact for Safe, Orderly and Regular Migration (GCM) is an inter-governmentally negotiated agreement that claims to cover 'all dimensions of international migration in a holistic and comprehensive manner'. Drafted and prepared under the auspices of the United Nations, it is, fortunately for Europe, not legally binding (under international law). Its contents have caused great controversy and many countries have refused to sign and implement it, as this could undermine their efforts to protect their own borders.

only come to pass thanks to a minority of differentiated, lucid and combative men who will fight without any soul-searching. I could, of course, be wrong and Guillaume right. The very near future will tell, and we will not have to wait too long to find out. In the absence of a revolutionary awakening, however, we will all be condemned to physically disappear, unless we choose to flee to an Eastern European country.

A Multifaceted Talent

Guillaume Faye's genius was expressed in different ways and at different times. The very structure of his thoughts was, however, a homogeneous one. Whatever some may have thought, he never contradicted himself.

Based on the strategic choices he made throughout his life and the ideas he always hammered home in his work, one can notice an evolution that took place from top to bottom, i.e. from ideological concepts to the reality on the ground. Guillaume Faye was a field activist: the sole purpose of his work is, ultimately, to suggest emergency solutions and define the necessary methods that would enable their realistic and effective implementation. Guillaume declared himself a follower of Aristotle, the philosopher for whom everything was subject to demonstration.

Guillaume dedicated himself to many (often very different) activities and excelled in every single one.

He was, above all else, a brilliant and passionate orator: his often-improvised speech was marked by flashes of sheer brilliance, which he himself discovered at the very same moment the public did and which aroused awe within him as well. Most speakers need to follow a set pattern, which is definitely my case, as I cannot speak without having any notes at my disposal; otherwise, I forget half of what I have promised myself to say. By contrast, a piece of paper was always enough for

Guillaume, and it must be said that I never saw him begin a lecture without a good helping of his favourite fuel, i.e. beer or wine.

During a period that lasted for ten whole years, from 1987 to 1997, Guillaume worked as *a radio host* going by the name of Skyman, as well as a *television host* on France 2, where he came up with various pranks in the programme *Télématin*. During that same period, he also participated in *comic book* magazines such as *L'Écho des savanes*, in the company of more or less insane authors, who, more often than not, belonged to the extreme-left spectrum.

He would resume his activism as *a lecturer, a journalist and a writer* upon returning to G.R.E.C.E. in 1997, following a ten-year separation from the latter. Regarding his literary activity, apart from his truly numerous articles published in the movement's various magazines, he authored twenty-eight books in three different periods, the first lasting from 1981 to 1987. The second took place outside the metapolitical sphere and stretched from 1987 to 1997. As for the third, it began in 1998 and lasted until his death. In 2000, he would, once again, be excluded from G.R.E.C.E., as a result of the publication of his book entitled *La colonisation de l'Europe*, which was allegedly deemed too politically incorrect by G.R.E.C.E. leaders.

There is a chronological logic to be found in the development of his literary production. Indeed, the first period corresponds to the elaboration of a doctrinal corpus through his first book, *Le système à tuer les peoples* (published in 1981), and a very interesting booklet entitled *L'Occident comme déclin*, which was released in 1984. As for the second period, it is of less interest, unless one is a comic book enthusiast.

The third period would see Faye come out all guns blazing with *L'Archéofuturisme* and the first pamphlets targeting Islam, including *La colonisation de l'Europe*, originally published in 2000. In his last book, *La guerre civile raciale*, these pamphlets would become an entire indictment against the invasion of Europe at the hands of the Muslim masses arriving from the Maghreb and sub-Saharan/black Africa.

Guillaume's mind would follow the development of this situation most closely and he would react like a general on a battlefield, a general who had mastered all the factors, minute by minute, and had made decisions which most of his subordinates were unable to understand. His readers and friends were often taken aback by what they believed to be sudden about-turns, which they were not, however. Guillaume Faye always waged attacks in the exact places where defences had weakened and where they needed to be reinforced. Little by little, and with the precision of a 'surgical strike', he pinpointed the gravest danger, pushing aside the remaining ones and advocating temporary alliances, especially with Israel, which was not to everyone's liking. He thus highlighted the danger to which one had to turn all of their attention and efforts, namely the Great Replacement of the European populations at the hands of African populations that were being manipulated and united by the Muslim religion. In his last book, which was published posthumously, Guillaume no longer makes any distinction between Islam and Islamism, and thus uses the generic term 'Muslim' instead.[10] I bought his last book from Daniel Conversano, who, having been Guillaume's final publisher, took it out of the trunk of his car, inside the perimeter of the cemetery where Guillaume had been interred. This was yet another way to pay homage to him.

The Main Themes in Guillaume Faye's Works

One can extract several main themes from the work of Guillaume Faye, themes which he bore within him throughout his life and repeated in almost every single book and speech. It is a permanent feature or constant that is found in all artists and authors that have a message to convey: they thus hammer it home so that it becomes well-imprinted in people's minds and permeates their eyes and ears. As for

---

10   TN: This was already the case in *Understanding Islam*, but Mr Blairon has not read it yet.

us, we have adopted most of these topics, which thus embody the very essence of our struggles and conversations.

The fight against standardisation and globalism — In the 1970s, it was mainly the United States that imposed upon us its commercial dictates and its society of endless disposability. The reign of quantity had spread across the entire planet.

The Left-Right divide that still existed at the turn of the previous century is no longer appropriate, for we have realised that the struggle actually involves two opposing extremes: the globalists on one side and the identitarians on the other; our world's standardisation versus the preservation of our territories; nature versus the artificial; and localism versus the 'zonification' of spaces.

Europe — In Guillaume Faye's eyes, Europe is not merely the power that has shaped the world through its creativity and technological ingenuity. Indeed, thanks to the very diversity of its own peoples, it also acts as the last flag-bearer of the white world. The first thing one had to do was to clearly distinguish the western world, which would become that of a *Big Brother* paving the way for a global government, from the world of tradition, which dates back thousands of years and retains the roots without which nothing can grow. And it was Faye who, more than anyone else, drew the line that separates the two. Our Europe is not that of Brussels, which only relays the above-mentioned globalism, but the true Europe of blood and soil, that of the white world which stands against the grey world of globalists, merchants and slaves.

Ethno-masochism — This term was actually coined by Guillaume himself and has become part of our language, although perhaps not the common one. It is, instead, part of the language of awareness, the language of all those who wish to clearly define behaviours. Europeans have been subjected to intensive propaganda, which consists in stripping them of all feelings of pride in their own history, their culture, their heritage, the beauty of their peoples, the beauty of their creations, the beauty of their women, and the beauty of their landscapes;

of all beauty, plain and simple. They have fallen into this morbid trap, one whose sole purpose is to bring about their gradual disappearance, depriving them of all reasons to live and driving them to the point of suicide, as is the case for our farmers.

The convergence of catastrophes — Following in the footsteps of the French mathematician René Thom, Guillaume Faye substantiated the threat of a convergence of catastrophes comprising demographic disasters, epidemics, natural disasters, wars, famines, ecological disasters, the suicide of entire peoples, etc.

This convergence of catastrophes actually has older roots if we look further back in time, at the sacred history of the gods rather than man's recent history (i.e. profane history). All ancient traditions whose basis is a cyclical one have mentioned this type of ultimate catastrophes in the past; to ascertain this, all one has to do is read Eliade, Daniélou, Evola or Guénon. In the eyes of our elders, a convergence of catastrophes manifests itself through a conjunction of astrological cycles, as the small ones interlock with the large ones and, at a certain moment, all come together to reach an end before starting again, just like the hands of a watch come together at the 6th dial (i.e. 666) and then continue at different speeds. Guillaume had, incidentally, surprised me by quoting one of my articles on the subject in his *Convergence des catastrophes*, which he had signed with his pseudonym, Corvus. I do not know if he did that because he wanted to make me happy, but I doubt that he was genuinely convinced by the constant references to ancient traditions comprised in that text. It was an article taken from *Roquefavour* magazine, which I myself published at the time, an article that actually dated back to 2004 and was subsequently included in my book *La Roue et le sablier*.[11]

Archeofuturism — According to what he himself stated on the back cover of this book (published in 1998), *L'Archéofuturisme* is, to Guillaume, '*a book which reveals that our roots only have a future if we*

---

11   TN: The Wheel and the Hourglass.

can transform them and project them into the latter'. What we have here
is an intellectually elaborate image of a natural process: simply put,
the fate of a tree that needs its own roots to grow and become more
beautiful through its leaves and flowers, or, alternatively, a reference
to the first human invention: the notion of a wheel, a world in motion
that revolves around a stationary core, the guardian of eternal values.
Politically, we can compare the concept of Archeofuturism with that
of a conservative-revolutionary stance, which may, at first sight, seem
contradictory but is in fact the very condition of human life.

It should, furthermore, be noted that Julius Evola participated, as
a futurist painter, in the eponymous movement created by the Italian
painter Marinetti.

Technoscience — Guillaume extolled the virtues of technoscience.
The fact is that it was Europe that gave the world its technology, i.e. a
kind of artificial prosthesis intended to replace attributes that men do
not (or no longer) naturally have. This technological frenzy has invad-
ed every single sphere of our lives, from the smallest household appli-
ances to *Ariane* rockets, in conditions that were not always regulated
by the sense of measure which Guillaume, as a disciple of Socrates,
was so very fond of. And this last statement is definitely truthful,
even if some may smile about it. Guillaume had developed a kind of
romantic, pre-transhumanist philosophy that exalted this European
technological genius, but had, in doing so, erased the very real danger of the transhumanist scheme aimed at transforming man into a
robot that would follow the orders of a few mad scientists financed by
certain billionaires, who are just as disturbed and govern the planet.
He, likewise, championed the super-humanist and promethean values
that have, alas, ushered us into the cold technocracy of our elites and
the soulless gigantism of our cities.

Islam — Throughout his work, Guillaume clearly designated Islam
as our primary enemy, an enemy that one had to rid themselves of
most urgently; for Islam is not merely a religion. What it is, in fact, is
the embodiment of an entire totalitarian system that regulates each

and every action performed by Muslim believers and is fuelled by a proselytising mission that aims to submit the whole planet to its beliefs; which defines Islam as a dangerous sect.

Guillaume's Life

All that is left is for me to talk about Guillaume's life, which was anything but a long and tranquil river.

Here is what I wrote in an article published after his passing:

> He was a meteor, burning his life away in a thousand flashes of light. Indeed, a meteor is a celestial body that never falls to the earth's surface and disappears once consumed.

Despite coming from the great bourgeoisie, he would quickly reject all 'conformist and materialist ideals', as he himself said. From then on, his life would continually be exposed to jealousy and endless injunctions to toe the line; for *our good people do not appreciate it when others follow a different path to theirs*, as Georges Brassens[12] once sang. It must be said that Guillaume Faye gave quarter neither to the bourgeoisie nor to his various critics and censors; and none of them ever failed to reciprocate.

He had earned a degree in political sciences and had quickly become involved in metapolitics, as he was barely twenty-one years old when Dominique Venner invited him to join G.R.E.C.E. in 1970 — which means that he never actually had the possibility to even consider leading an orderly life devoid of material worries, the kind of life that his keen intelligence and deeply cultured mind would easily have taken to great heights. Did he, however, desire such a peaceful life?

The only time when he could have conciliated the System was in 1986, when his argument with G.R.E.C.E. leaders led to their going

---

12   TN: Georges Charles Brassens (22nd October, 1921–29th October, 1981) was a French singer-songwriter and poet.

their separate ways and to the commencement of his showbiz parenthesis. Never was he willing to pass under the yoke[13] of the world he
hated, and if he did so on this occasion, it was only in a parodic way, so
as to deride it and ridicule all those who contributed to its durability.

According to the extensive article which Robert Steuckers has
just published on Guillaume, those who had asked him to dedicate
himself body and soul to G.R.E.C.E. allegedly rewarded him with a
minimum wage that would never allow him to indulge in any 'fancies'
whatsoever; to which I add that it was not his book sales that enabled
him to live decently. It was, however, a state of affairs that he accepted,
as it enabled him to partly develop his own ideas and accomplish his
mission.

Indeed, our movement was very quick to notice Guillaume's genius, his capacity to reinvent the world at every moment, to adapt to its
vagaries and to harmoniously integrate into its perpetual movement,
which constitutes one of the major characteristics of the Celtic culture,
whose outlines Jean Markale[14] had so well perceived. Guillaume Faye
was born on 7th November, 1949 in Angoulême, which is located in

---

13   TN: Forcing one's enemies to 'pass under the yoke' (Latin: *sub iugum*) was a
      ritual act of humiliation practiced by the peoples of ancient Italy, especially the
      Romans and Samnites. On a linguistic level, what is interesting to note is that
      the modern English terms 'subjugate' and 'subjugation' are actually rooted in
      the Latin phrase '*sub iugum*'.

14   TN: Jean Bertrand (23rd May, 1928–23rd November, 2008), otherwise known
      under his pen name Jean Markale, was a French author, poet, radio show
      host, lecturer and high school French teacher who lived in Brittany. He wrote
      many books centred around various subjects such as the summation of various
      myths; the latter's connection with topics such as the Templars, the Cathars and
      the Rennes le Château mystery; Atlantis; Druidism and the megalith-building
      civilisations; and the biography of (Saint) Columba.

the Charente region, the land of the Celtic Santones[15] and Petrocorii.[16] According to Pierre Vial and Robert Steuckers, Guillaume's two successive separations from G.R.E.C.E. had actually traumatised him, though he never broached the subject with me — perhaps out of modesty? His impulsive nature may have led him to hurt certain people through his fiery reactions, but he quickly became aware of this and regretted his behaviour. He then became a fragile and vulnerable lad who should have been protected, not overburdened. This is what Pierre Vial wrote about him:

> Once the divorce with certain hierarchs of the New Right had become inevitable, it impacted the very depths of his being, though only few of us ever realised it. There were wounds in him that never fully healed, and the excesses that he succumbed to were thus largely due to this plight of his — of this I am convinced.

Steuckers adds:

> [...] Vial, using a few perfectly crafted sentences, managed to put his finger on the very profundity of the psychological problem that had burdened Faye's person, on this unspeakable, immense and incurable sadness that had slowly transformed him and condemned the generous, happy and curious boy he was to becoming a man who, for ten whole years, had fallen prey to a farce, which he longed to free himself of, a man who had aged prematurely and been undermined by a most insidious evil.

And it is, once again, Robert Steuckers who shall allow me to have the last word, as he was the one who pointed out the fact that Guillaume

---

15   TN: The Santones, Santoni or Santii were a tribe that inhabited the part of ancient Gaul located in the modern region of Saintonge, around the city of Saintes. Beginning in the 1ˢᵗ century BC, the Romans would proceed to invade and occupy this Santone territory.

16   TN: The Petrocorii were a small tribe that lived along the northern bank of the Garunna (the Garonne river) in south-western Gaul. They were surrounded by the Santones to the north-west, the Lemovices to the north-east, the Cadurci to the east, the Nitiobroges to the south and the Biturices to the west.

had been buried in the cemetery of the old village in whose municipal area the *Futuroscope* site is actually located. Archeo-futurism — quite symbolic, wouldn't you say?

In the eyes of his friends, Guillaume shall always remain the benevolent and cheerful companion, whose fragile yet fiery destiny they all tried to preserve, to the best of their abilities.

End Theme

The God 'Ethnos'

By Pierre Krebs

To Guillaume —

    for our fraternity in our common struggle, here below,
     and the one to come in the age of the Elsewhere,
    as decided by the gods of Olympus
     and those of Walhalla.
    There are some men exalted by fate
    above all others, in a tempest state,
    like a sign of the times in which they exist,
    as the gods' elect sentries, they endure and persist
    to ensure the survival of the blood and essence
    of their ancestors, now threatened with evanescence.

    On they go through the raging storm
    and amidst its squalls are transformed
    by the cosmic Wind's purifying life-breath.
    They melt into the cold watery depths
    and are transformed within the hagal
    ice of cosmic Memory's preserving realm of crystal.

    They have stricken the Earth's vessel
    that lies at the feet of Yggdrasil
    with the tempest's flashes and jolts,
    and have dissolved themselves in the will
    to power born of regenerating cosmic firebolts.

    They have rendered the sky's canopy weak,
    the arch perched upon Yggdrasil's peak,
    within the rumbling thunder of the storm
    and amidst the earth's song to transform,
    illuminating cosmic Order to reform.

    'Twas water and air,

thunder and fiery glare
that then chiselled into the tablets of history
their teachings' very own breviary,
forever carved in their memory
and which neither the old decaying ages
nor the capricious war that the world upon them wages
shall ever manage to erase
from the awakened minds of the men of their race.

For the wisdom that they breathe
shall unfailingly cross the barriers of Time
 and unto further generations of sentinels bequeath,
in the uninterrupted cyclic phases
of dawns that follow eventides,
the transcendent wisdom of the god Ethnos
and his vitalist and super-humanist enlightenment
which, since the origin of all ages and species, has bestowed
upon all the peoples of our terrestrial abode
the unveiling of the spirit and the world's re-enchantment,
through the inescapable laws defined
by the only eternity whose name is known to us:
heredity according to the races.

PIERRE KREBS,
30th April, 2019

Annexes

A Review of Guillaume Faye's
Système à tuer les peuples

Initially published in Renaissance européenne, *issue number 38, summer of* 1981.

MASSIFICATION. Depersonalisation. Is this still civilisation? No, replies Guillaume Faye, it is the system. For whereas a civilisation remains endowed with a sense of continuity, the system is mechanical and timeless, lacking any and all inner life.

The system's premises are a challenge that the dominant ideologies of the so-called 'Western' world have not been able to meet. The system has spread across the entire planet and appears to us in the threefold form of supranational technoeconomic structures, a universalist (and paradoxically mercantile and bureaucratic) ideology, and 'US-Western' mass culture. Certain nations, such as Denmark, the Netherlands and Greece, for instance, are subject, more than others, to the process of being consumed by this American-Western complex. The petty bourgeois mentality, which homogenises these populations, longs to acquire global proportions. Soon, men shall no longer know where they are and shall forget their own nations. Dominant forms of life shall slowly marginalise our values of belonging, our roots and our lineage, and these values shall then be 'folklorised', 'ornamentalised' and transformed into a smoke screen that conceals the 'progress' of planetary homogenisation; they shall simply be a source of entertainment.

In his very famous work entitled *Le bourgeois*,[1] which was published by Payot in 1966, Werner Sombart writes that the mercantile mindset is much more 'internationalist' than the Communist International; for what it fears above all are the upheavals of history, those triggered by men of faith and men of war. The only thing that the mercantile spirit longs to experience is practical immediacy, as it considers history to have already ended. The ardour of revolutionary messianism thus clashes with this 'last man' mentality. Now that the world has become a post-revolutionary one, there is no longer any room for great deeds and great epics.

One could indeed cast doubt upon the sustainability of such a scheme, and with good reason. Islamic awakening, the geopolitical game played by the Soviet Union, and the unemployment that plagues the industrial zones of Europe might very well upset this pleasant state of tranquillity. The mercantile system has, however, failed to anticipate this. Is the homogenisation it foresees inevitable? And if the answer is a negative one, what should we suggest instead?

As there is no longer anything left to distinguish peoples from each other, we await the advent of the '*homo oeconomicus*', of the figure that shall represent the economic-cultural complex — henceforth, cultural behaviour shall be equated to purchases, consumption choices, and economic preferences. Economy and (sub-)culture are very closely interlinked. All fashions, regardless of whether they pertain to clothing, food or music, exist because of people's interest in opening markets. To ensure that the latter become as large as possible, it is necessary to gradually eradicate the specific mores and traditions that could act as an obstacle to planetary standardisation *within* the mercantile system. And this standardisation has its own model: America. Indeed, the space in which culture is considered a mere 'product' is, linguistically, an Anglo-Saxon one, a space where the English language has already ventured very far from its own origins and has distanced itself

---

1   TN: The Bourgeois.

from its own myths; it has thus become extremely impoverished, even sterilised. This culture-product is what allows colonisation to occur from a distance. Thanks to it, America can be present everywhere. The lifestyle of the American petty bourgeoisie is thus becoming global. Nowadays, although the economic hegemony of the United States is experiencing a decline, the proliferation of so-called 'American styles' is not receding by any means; for colonised nations have turned themselves into actual providers of the system's mental and economic structures, of the Americano-sphere, so to speak. How are we to designate our enemy from now on? Indeed, does the danger not lie in the future impossibility of accusing the United States of being the sole creator and disseminator of Americanism? 'America is within us' is a truly alarming formula, and were it to ever prove completely true, it would indicate that we are already among the living dead…

The essence of the System is of a strictly economic and technological nature, and it can thus gradually rid itself of all traditional forms of political domination. The System no longer requires any leaders; what it needs, instead, are regulators. The political decisions taken by states are therefore replaced by strategic choices made within the framework of various networks — those of large companies, banking organisations, public or private speculators, etc. All these separate strategies trigger a *self-regulation* mechanism that allows the System to work towards satisfying its own ends, with no other purpose than its own growth. It is liberal and anti-authoritarian ideology that declares itself true to the *rationality* that justifies the System. As for Guillaume Faye, he denounces this ideology as being subtly totalitarian, for it presents itself as being the only option, *without any other alternative*. The ones who espouse the System's liberal-technocratic and self-regulating ideology genuinely believe in the *inevitability* of such *planetarisation*.[2]

The System's comprehensive management thus implies internal depoliticisation, which, in turn, presupposes the fact that societies are to

---

2   TN: A term that should be considered synonymous with 'globalisation'.

be stripped of any and all capacity for self-perception. And herein lies the tragic irony: the 'open society', which liberalism claims to embody, actually serves to transform populations into disoriented masses and 'opacifies' cultures. According to what Guillaume Faye writes, however, this is not to be understood as a derailment of liberalism, as a denial of its own ideological foundations. For its founding fathers are not innocent by any means. The System's totalitarian path is, in fact, paved with humanitarian concepts. Benjamin Constant, Adam Smith, and Thomas Paine already believed that everything that is historical, political, deep-rooted, sovereign, imperial and popular is supposed to involve risks that are likely to stray into immoralism. Therefore, it is indeed the merchant mindset that gives rise to the complete negation of the state. As a result, Marxism is actually less 'revolutionary': it leads to nationalism and the means that it has endowed itself with have only served to neutralise its ends.

This elimination of the historic heritage of all peoples results in the absolutisation of an ideological minimum, namely that of 'human rights'. The System entertains the hope that the latter will, in future, become the sole common ethical denominator. Even revolutionary Marxism has become incapable of denouncing bourgeois humanitarian law (in the name of proletarian impetuosity).

The 'egalitarian' ideology is reduced to the defence and illustration of *this new decalogue;*[3] we shall thus, from now on, be able to observe the end of its *inventive phase.* Former Trotskyites and Maoists have relinquished the dynamism of *'permanent revolution'* so as to regroup within the new 'sacred union', which centres around the 'religion' of human rights. The System thus 'digests' revolutionaries.

This absence of genuine revolutionary challenges creates what is commonly termed *'macro-stability'.* It may well be that the 'acceleration of history' is now a thing of the past. Over the past fifteen years, we have witnessed a stabilisation of ideological and geostrategic

---

3   TN: Capitalised, the term 'Decalogue' refers to the Bible's Ten Commandments.

configurations. These two historical-political fields are, however, not the only ones in this case. Modern art, for instance, has failed to invent anything since the rise of cubism and abstractionism at the turn of the century. The new narrative was a short-lived one. No new ideology has imposed itself upon the political 'market': liberals, ultra-conservatives, social democrats and Marxists all repeat the same themes, as if they were in an incantatory trance. Here and there, sociologists will, of course, spot a few rare quantitative developments — the presence of fewer peasants, an increase in the number of 'suburbanites', etc. As for television, it only accentuates a divide that dates back to the first decade of the current century.[4] From an international perspective, the Bandung Conference[5] (1955) did not change anything about the division that resulted from the Yalta Conference(1945);[6] for there has been no reversal in the balance of power. It was the dissident Baudrillard who used the right words: *this civilisation is no longer a 'modern' one, despite its cult of all that is 'new' — it is merely 'current'*. Within macro-stability, only micro-variations can ever occur. Trends are reversed and change, as seen in the case of cars and their radiator grilles or chrome plating, yet the direction in which our lives are heading remains, unfortunately, immutable.

---

4   TN: The 20th century.

5   TN: The Bandung Conference was the very first large-scale Asian–African (or Afro–Asian) conference to be held. It was, in fact, a meeting of Asian and African states that had, for the most part, only recently claimed their independence. The conference's official purpose was to promote Afro-Asian economic and cultural cooperation and reject any and all forms of colonialism or neo-colonialism.

6   TN: The Yalta Conference, also known as the Crimea Conference and code-named the Argonaut Conference, took place from the 4th to the 11th of February, 1945, and can be regarded as *the* World War II meeting that brought together the heads of government of the United States, the United Kingdom, and the Soviet Union to debate the restructuring of both Germany and Europe in the post-war period. Due to various personal antagonisms and objections, General de Gaulle — and thus France itself — was excluded from attendance.

Culture has become a drawer in which one respectfully stores everything that is not 'current' and therefore useless. We are experiencing a nostalgia that the System will organise and render profitable. Any re-rooting is channelled through lesser, decorative means of evocation or restoration, so that it cannot give birth to any action-bearing myth. In Guillaume Faye's eyes, *there is a gap that separates the System from Life itself*, a gap that lies between the System and all that is not part of it. This antithesis covers a more fundamental antagonism than the old Left-vs-Right, socialism-vs-liberalism or materialism-vs-idealism divide. Consequently, new political regroupings will eventually have to take place, and shall come to pass during the next century. Guillaume Faye's book is thus an appeal for Europeans to act. *The peoples of Europe must cease to confuse the Western System with their civilisation's values and destiny.* In actual fact, the only position that is truly revolutionary and can assert itself in the face of the system does not stem from any old ideologies. Instead, it belongs to those who contest the system's very essence, its ethical and ideological bases and its 'genealogy' — meaning *those who fight for the cause of peoples against a standardised global society*; those who champion a fighting spirit and a sense of destiny in the face of the egalitarian alienation of economic happiness; and those who support national, regional or cultural forces against bourgeois cosmopolitanism, which longs to reign over dead peoples in a totalitarian fashion.

ROBERT STEUCKERS

Guillaume Faye's Gun-Like Quill

Pierre Krebs' preface to the German edition of Why We Fight — Manifesto of the European resistance (*Wofür wir kämpfen. Manifest des europäischen Widerstandes. Das metapolitische Hand- und Wörterbuch der kulturellen Revolution zur Neugeburt Europas*, Ahnenrad der Moderne, Kassel-Horn-Bad Wildungen, 2006).

The Great Dress Rehearsal
Announced by Giorgio Locchi

IN TIMES OF LIES and cowardice, truth and courage are regarded as capital mistakes, and the rare writers insane enough to dare challenge the former as dangerous heretics. And lo and behold, a writer of the race of the Great Heretics has come to us during the most deceptive and cowardly period of our entire history so as to give us a most lucid and most courageous demonstration of the fact that this 'peace' is but a veneer that masks the most deceitful, most vicious and most dangerous 'state of war' that may well cause Europe's demise should our continent not manage to revive its resistance and survival instincts — with the obvious and implicit understanding that what is also hanging in the balance is the survival or disappearance of the culture of which its peoples are the genitors.

But what decline, dangers, and demise is Europe actually threatened with? Akin to legendary dragons, this decline, these perils and this death all lie in wait in the shape of many-headed monsters.[1] The loss of the values that have forged European culture already shows the true extent of its decline. These values include community belonging; identity-based, ethnic and historical awareness; meritocracy; selectivity; elitism and the exaltation of the best; organic democracy; superhumanism; will to power; and a sense of honour. We can detect the above-mentioned perils at all levels of Europe's political, cultural and social hierarchy — Americanism, cosmopolitanism, consumerism and mercantilism, devirilisation, homosexuality, egalitarianism, the reign of the mercantile society and of the *homo oeconomicus*, presentism, ethno-masochism, universalism and globalism, xenophilia, and individualism. At the end of this mental, spiritual and political path of degeneration, death reveals its presence under Europe's demographic collapse, behind the colonisation and settlement conducted by both non-indigenous masses and Islam, and underneath the time bomb of ethnic chaos and interbreeding.

Contrary to the suicidal ideological positions espoused by the sorcerer's apprentices[2] of a multiracial society, the analyses carried out by experts in matters of immigration, demography or the economy are symptomatic of the growing chasm that increasingly separates the clairvoyance of scientists from the dementia of mobster politicians. Professor Herwig Birg, the head of the Institute for Population Research at the University of Bielefeld, is adamant in his position:

---

1   TN: Although the author uses the generic term 'dragons', it is clear that 'hydra' would have been more adequate. Indeed, the Hydra (of Lerna) was, in Greek and even Roman mythology, a serpentine/dragon-like monster displaying many heads. It was notoriously difficult to slay, as each of its heads would regrow upon being severed from its neck. Let us sincerely hope, however, that the comparison the author and I (by extension, of course) have drawn remains inaccurate. For Europe's sake.

2   TN: Meaning by those who would love to magically establish a well-functioning society where all races would somehow manage to co-exist in harmony.

Our country is becoming a third-world state. And I say this very consciously (...) If this mass immigration at the hands of third-world countries is not brought to a halt, Germany risks losing everything — a culture that is globally held in great esteem and the social well-being which rests upon that culture.[3]

He, furthermore, predicts a disastrous scenario for the coming four years:

In our major German cities, the majority of the population will, in 2010, be comprised of immigrants below the age of forty. In a mocking display of irony, fate does indeed supplant all scenarios when one imagines that, having been catapulted into the position of our country's new masters, yesterday's "guest-workers"[4] shall henceforth find themselves in a position of power.

Birg then adds unflinchingly:

It shall "then be important to our compatriots" to gain, as much as at all possible, their former "guests'" sympathy, to do everything they can to ensure that the latter "do not harbour any aggressive feelings whatsoever towards the Germans"![5]

In plain and simple English, these words amount to the following: the Germans will have to determine very quickly what the best methods are that would guarantee that they are viewed positively by foreigners — if, of course, they truly want the latter to agree to tolerate the presence of Germans in their own country.

---

3   AN: Herwig Birg, *Aus Politik und Zeitgeschichte* number 20, 2003.

4   TN: In Germany, the term that is used in connection with foreign workers is 'Gastarbeiter'. It initially referred to the foreign/migrant workers that had come to West Germany between the years of 1955 and 1973 in search of employment, within the framework of an official guest-worker programme. One wonders whether the professor's prediction with regard to the year of 2010 proved accurate in the end.

5   *Frankfurter Allgemeine Sonntagszeitung*, 1st April, 2006.

It is a well-known fact that decadence always costs more than prosperity. The billions taken out of the wealth that was previously accumulated through the work of our peoples serve, so to speak, as bank cards to be used by the conmen of multiracialism, who thus finance crimes using the victims' money. For we are truly financing our own walk towards the scaffold and voluntarily giving our hangmen the highest possible pay. Yes, indeed — *Europe is giving its wealth away so as to fund its own suicide*. Economic ruin thus heralds the genetic bankruptcy of our peoples who, conditioned to a point where they can no longer react, hide behind the increasingly thin shadow of their own silhouette.

In another visionary work, the most clairvoyant, most fruitful and most radical thinker of the 'New Culture' revisits the imminence of danger and the increasingly urgent necessity of identitarian revival, which acts as the very foundation of Resistance and Reconquest:

> Could what the philosopher Giorgio Locchi told me some time before his passing thus turn out to be true? Indeed, he warned me that the last world war was going to have its logical consequences and had actually only been a dress rehearsal; that Greater Europe — which, to me, is Euro-Siberia — was still going to suffer the final assault conducted by all coalesced peoples. Giorgio Locchi posited that, in war, no defeat is actually definitive and truly decisive. He believed in the construction of our Great Fatherland and thought that revenge was still possible, as was final victory, even if we seemed to have fallen to the very bottom of the abyss. Steeped in Italo-Roman tradition and that Germanic soul which, although now hidden, is still very much alive, Giorgio Locchi asked me to continue this work, in my own, French way, i.e. with a *furia francese*. Rarely encountered in France nowadays, the latter is nonetheless alive among certain Gallic elites and consists of resisting by attacking mercilessly, fearlessly, pitilessly, and without resorting to any circumlocutions, sloppy mistakes, customary precautions or intellectual jargons. The War has only just begun, and we shall have to ride the tiger.[6] Locchi had also warned me that the worst enemies

---

6   TN: *Ride the Tiger: A Survival Manual for the Aristocrats of the Soul* is considered one of Julius Evola's greatest works. His concept of 'riding the tiger' refers

were embodied by false friends, informers, thieves and distorters of ideas, spies and soul manipulators, who lurk, concealed, at the very heart of our own camp. The great confrontation is now imminent and will either be synonymous with our death or equivalent to our rebirth. Whatever the case, it may well represent our very last chance.[7]

Guillaume Reinstates Words in their Context of Accuracy, Allowing Ideas to Reclaim their Rightful Place

Why We Fight is a book which undoubtedly belongs to the tradition of the great awakeners of the People. Due to its uncompromising description of a reality that has virtually been drained of all hope, it is an upsetting sort of book. On the other hand, however, it is also a cathartic book, thanks to its description of the means and action strategies that Europe still has at its disposal and which may yet free it from the arms of death — as long as Europeans are aware of this fact, and under the condition that they will it so and act accordingly. There are some ideas in this book that can thus awaken the spirit of European resistance, in addition to certain means that can unite Europeans once and for all, from the coast of Iceland to the edge of Siberia. And that's not all: what the book contains is, above all, a re-definition of key concepts in which this rebirth might be rooted; an immensely extensive project which was to include the drafting of a basic *Dictionary* comprising one hundred and seventy-seven keywords [to which we added two terms, namely *ethnocracy* and *genopolitics*, Pierre Krebs notes] and which only the poly-morphic mind of Guillaume Faye, ever active in the service of a multi-talented intelligence, could ever have undertaken and brought to fruition.

---

to the ability of certain select people to harness a destructive power and turn it into a source of inner liberation, thus giving hope to all those who long to re-espouse Tradition.

7   AN: Guillaume Faye, *Avant-Guerre. Chronique d'un cataclysme annoncé*, L'Æncre, Paris, 2002. The quoted text has been rendered slightly more concise.

It should indeed be known that the System that has been dis-
mantling Europe acts in an ethno-masochistic manner worthy of a
Derrida,[8] the philosopher of a linguistic deconstruction that verbally
destroyed traditions, institutions and laws before arriving at the destruction of the world, plain and simple. From the deconstruction
of language, the System moved on to the deconstruction of identity-
related meanings, and from the latter kind of deconstruction to the
outright eradication of both territories and peoples.

The *quill* that wrote this book is therefore also a *gun* that has managed to hit the bull's eye on all the targets of European decadence,
beginning with those that relate to language, thus gunning down
false ideas and erasing all the confusion, all the semantic perversions,
all the false statements and all the fake values that they produce and
whose immediate consequence is that of anaesthetising our wills and,
subsequently, paralysing our identity instincts. It is, likewise, a book of
ideas, ideas which did not sprout from the reveries of a fanciful brain,
but, on the contrary, germinated and grew from the author's cold and
lucid observation of the worst political, cultural or sociological realities of an era that is being devoured by the ogres of decadence; ideas
which, above all, are now poised to spout out of the daring brains that
shall awaken new wills capable of delivering our people's increasingly
cadaverous masses from the gigantic seraglio[9] of this putrefaction-
breeding era.

---

8   TN: Born Jackie Élie Derrida, Jacques Derrida (15th July, 1930–9th October,
     2004) was an Algerian-born French philosopher. He is most famous for hav-
     ing formulated a type of semiotic analysis termed 'deconstruction', which he
     expanded on in several texts, all within a context of phenomenology. Derrida
     is, furthermore, one of the principal figures associated with post-structuralism
     and postmodern philosophy.

9   TN: I believe that the author has, once again, purposely opted for this specific
     word to convey two simultaneous meanings. Indeed, the word 'seraglio' can
     be interpreted as a Turkish/Ottoman palace or court, which alludes to notions
     of invasion at the hands of Muslim masses (since such a place should not
     be present on French soil). Additionally, however, the term can also refer to

On the other hand, we can thus better understand why the *reconquering of ideas* necessarily entails the *reconquering of words* and the *re-appropriation* of their actual meaning. For one cannot awaken instincts without, first of all, dissipating the mental confusion that renders the mind disoriented; nor can one *re-establish order* in the world without first *re-arranging* concepts, or *re-orient* the mind without first cleansing words of all the false utterances that pervert their meaning — a fact which Bernhard Kummer, a Germanist and specialist in religious matters, understood perfectly when he wrote:

> Whoever understands the racial laws of our soul better than we do has the ability to lead us wherever he wants to.[10]

This implies that we must mount permanent counterattacks and ceaselessly wage war against the numerous and everyday acts of aggression and terrorism committed by the *politically correct*, as political correctness is but a ruse of war exploited by an enemy who is well aware of the fact that the most efficient means to lead the minds of a people astray — and thus weaken their resistance — lies in the corruption of their language. One thus had to reinstate words in their context of accuracy so as to allow ideas to spontaneously reclaim their rightful place. This is precisely what Guillaume Faye did by offering us, through this book of concepts, a manual of mental and semantic counterattack, i.e. the indispensable weapon that the European partisan still lacked to be able to thwart the extensive deculturation initiative targeting our peoples and acting as a preliminary stage of their genetic and identity-related annihilation.

---

a harem, in which case French people are understood as having become 'the sultan's harlots', existing only to serve their Muslim master(s). It is especially this second meaning that is appropriate in the above context of decadence.

10   AN: Bernhard Kummer, *Anfang und Ende des faustischen Jahrtausends*, Adolf Klein Verlag, Leipzig, 1934.

A Manual, a Reflection Tool, a Strategic Weapon, a Mental Compass and a Guide in the Struggle to Ignite the Fires of the Furia Europeana!

This book is much more than just that, for it serves as a manual; a reflection tool whose reading is absolutely necessary; a strategic weapon that one must brood over in a Nietzschean manner; a mental compass; a battle guide; and, last but not least, a basic reference for all the European identitarian forces of the 21ˢᵗ century. For this very reason, it is destined to become a milestone in the annals of our revival and rebirth.

Just like the previous work in this collection,[11] this book was penned out of a sense of duty, so as to obey the imperative necessities of a revival strategy and simultaneously serve as a corpus for a common European identitarian doctrine. Being *war books*, both act as a reminder of the fact that we are indeed in a state of war against an enemy that threatens to smother the very Essence of our Being, to snuff out our inalienable right to be and remain ourselves, in line with our ancestors whose biography has largely shaped the very history of the world, from the conquest of the Earth to that of the stars, in harmony with an age-old and absolute sort of respect for the laws of life, and against all criminal ideologies that strive to eradicate races and cultures through miscegenation. Both books are regarded as examples of supreme political and social *incorrectness* in the System's mobster-like understanding of things, since they are eminently *correct* from the perspective of the Right of Peoples and the laws of life that govern the latter.

Admittedly, the System still holds the cards in this political game, but what are the most sophisticated games worth without the trumps? Indeed, we have nothing but our own ideas, certainties and will, and thus very little in the face of the System's mind-shattering machinery,

---

11   AN: Pierre Krebs, *Im Kampf um das Wesen, Ahnenrad der Moderne*, Horn–Kassel, 1997. French edition published in 2002 by Pan Europa, Paris.

which crushes souls and destroys identities. And yet, we still have the best trump card in our possession, the ace of aces, one that they themselves lack and will never acquire, for they have clouded the pathways of blood beginning within themselves. As for us, we know where we are *heading* because we know where we have *come from*. We have, on our side, the Memory of History, which is the Memory of the Race Being; the awareness of belonging to an unbroken chain of ancestors who we still have the (the most exquisite) privilege to resemble.

Let us therefore put an end to debates that focus on issues that are mere details, i.e. on the problems of our *post*-renaissance! What we urgently require now are clear guidelines, intangible principles, indivertible values, and an unshakable faith in the latter — and it was Guillaume Faye who delineated them and redefined such values. For victory will always be claimed by those whose will and reason prove to be the strongest; and those whose actions abide by the principles of nature will always be in the right compared to those who destroy it! We shall be eternal as long as we uphold the law of ethnic homogeneity in the face of all reality-spurning schisms, as long as we stand by the miracle-law of blood, which replaces men without ever modifying them, the law that is governed by one of the rare gods whose name we know well: heredity!

Following the example of this book, which explains to us *Why We Fight*, thus restoring our sense of direction, reconstructing our foundations and projecting a certain vision of our future, let us all now strike the little match of the *furia francese* that Guillaume spoke of, as well as the *furia española, furia teutonica* and *furia italiana, russia, bulgaria, helvetica, croatia, islandia*, etc. Yes, indeed, that is when we shall manage to light the bonfire of the entire *furia europeana*, thanks to which the world shall, once again, be restored to health.

The challenge is a considerable one, but it is from this madness that wisdom is born, from this will that life is transmitted and from this despair that hope arises; for it is at the very epicentre of danger that the source of salvation keeps growing — as long, of course, as one is aware of it, believes in it and longs for it. For the sake of our now foolishly mindless peoples, we are prepared, if necessary, to follow in Nietzsche's footsteps and, wherever there are walls, inscribe eternal words that even the blind will be able to read, inescapable truths of the laws of blood that protect the Being of every single people and safeguard the Essence of each and every culture. For what now hangs in the balance, more than ever before, is the primordial fire of our own *genos*, the Being of our own *ethnos*, and the spinning wheel of our own *germen*, which lies at the source of our Soul and Spirit's very Being, each indissolubly bound to the other in the very Essence of the Race that engenders them.

Long live the New Will, so that the Race may endure and the Spirit be victorious!

PIERRE KREBS

Guillaume Faye and the Convergence of Catastrophes

An introduction made by Robert Steuckers during Guillaume Faye's presentation of his book La convergence des catastrophes, *which he signed Guillaume Corvus (Ravensteinhof, Brussels, 21ˢᵗ January, 2006)*

In the introduction to one of the Italian versions of Guillaume Faye's first book, *Le système à tuer les peuples*, I attempted to succinctly outline his political itinerary, starting from his student years at the IEP and the Sorbonne. I called to mind the influence exerted by Julien Freund, Pareto's theories and Bertrand de Jouvenel on this young student, whose mission would drive him to fight a metapolitical battle, first through the 'Spengler Circle' and then via G.R.E.C.E. (the Research and Study Group for European Civilisation) itself. I also concentrated on his interpretation of Nietzsche's ideas, in which, just like Alexis Philonenko,[1] he banked on a loud and altogether Rabelaisian sort of laughter, one that was simultaneously deconstructive and reconstructive, i.e. on a mockery which dissolves the certainties of the mediocre and the conformists. I am not going to repeat the entire content today, as it can all be read on the internet, but will mainly focus on a concept that is truly omnipresent in Faye's work, namely the cardinal notion of 'the political'; yes indeed, the very same 'notion of the political' so dear to Professor Julien Freund.

---

1   TN: Alexis Philonenko (21ˢᵗ May, 1932–12ᵗʰ September, 2018) was a French philosopher and historian of philosophy.

The domain of the political, and not that of (strict) politics, is the sphere of genuine issues, issues that are decisive with regard to the life and survival of a given political entity. What this life and survival permanently postulate is proper management and a good *'nomos* of the *oikos'* (to use Carl Schmitt's Greek terminology), wherein one permanently considers long-term matters and not only short-term ones and is never limited to an immediacy that lacks temporal depth nor to a repetitive sort of presentism that remains devoid of any and all foresight.

A good *nomos* is therefore one that ensures the survival of a political community, state or empire; one that generates, by means of the daily anticipation and far-sightedness that it entails, a large capital gain in every field; and one that leads to power in the good sense of the word. For power is nothing but one's solid capital of material and immaterial resources accumulated in anticipation of serious blows, backlashes or disasters. Such is the essential notion advocated by Clausewitz,[2] a man who is rather too hastily labelled an all-out warmonger. What Clausewitz focuses on above all else is the accumulation of resources that render war useless, since no enemy would dare to confront a well-fashioned polity,[3] or, alternatively, make one's political entity difficult or impossible to devour or put out of action. It is nothing more than an implementation of the ancient Roman adage which states that if one desires peace, one must prepare for war.[4]

---

2   TN: Carl Philipp Gottfried or Gottlieb von Clausewitz (1st June, 1780–16th November, 1831) was a Prussian general and military theorist who emphasised the 'moral' (i.e., in modern terms, psychological) and political aspects of war. He is most famous for having penned *Vom Kriege* (English: *On War*), which remained unfinished at the time of his death. Although generally regarded as a realist and somewhat of a romantic, Clausewitz was also largely inspired by the rationalist ideas of the European Enlightenment.

3   TN: i.e. a state defined as a political entity, an organised society.

4   TN: '*Si vis pacem, para bellum*', generally translated as 'if you want peace, prepare for war'.

The Immortal Work of Carl
Schmitt and Julien Freund

So, where does this notion of 'the political' actually come from? It stems, first of all, from the work of Carl Schmitt, in whose eyes it revolves around two truths that have been observed throughout history:

- The political is borne by a person of flesh and blood who makes decisions in a most responsible manner (Weber). The model advocated by Schmitt, a Rhenish Catholic man, is that of the papal institution, which decides both sovereignly and in the final instance, without ever being accountable to partial and partisan organisations, all of which are seditious, centrifugal and driven by specific and non-general behaviour-influencing desires and interests.

- The political sphere remains a solid one as long as the principle formulated by Thomas Hobbes[5] in the seventeenth century is abided by: '*Auctoritas non veritas facit legem*' (meaning that it is, in fact, authority, and not truth, that makes the law / defines the norm). Now that we stand at the threshold of this twenty-first century, which is likely to be a century of catastrophes, just like the previous one, we could indeed extend Hobbes' reflection on the matter and say: *Auctoritas non lex facit imperium*, i.e. that 'it is authority, not the law/norm, that makes empires'. By stressing Hobbes' notions of political science, what Schmitt strived to denounce was the danger of governing a state in accordance with abstract standards and hypothetical and paralysing principles, which sometimes act as vectors of calamitous dissensions that could lead to civil war. All it takes are a few decades of such

---

5   TN: Thomas Hobbes of Malmesbury (5th April, 1588–4th December, 1679) was an English philosopher. He is widely considered one of the founders of modern political philosophy, though his contributions actually span across other fields as well, including geometry, history, theology, ethics and jurisprudence.

governance and the 'Gordian knots' accumulate, plunging the polities that have revelled in it into a state of dangerous stagnation. What one thus requires are (personal or coactive) authorities that have the ability to disentangle or sever such 'Gordian knots'.

This notion of the political stems, furthermore, from the ideas expressed by Professor Julien Freund, a Strasbourgeois who was, admittedly, one of Carl Schmitt's best disciples. He adopted the notion and implemented it in a context that was very different to that of Weimar Germany or Nazism, focusing, instead, on Gaullist and post-Gaullist France, which were also a product of Carl Schmitt's thoughts. One should not, in fact, forget that René Capitant, the man who authored the 'presidentialist' constitution of our Fifth Republic, was actually Schmitt's first faithful French disciple. The President of the Fifth Republic is indeed an *auctoritas*, in the sense espoused by both Hobbes and Schmitt, deriving his legitimacy from the direct votes cast by the entire population. He must be a charismatic man of flesh and blood, one that everyone considers capable of making the right decisions at the right time. A disciple of Schmitt and Capitant, Julien Freund poured his reflections on this cardinal notion of the political into a small work that we were still made to read at the Saint-Louis University Faculties of Brussels some thirty years ago: *Qu'est-ce que le politique?*[6] (published by Editions du Seuil). The book has not aged one tiny bit and remains mandatory reading for all those who, within the political arena, still long to think clearly and straightforwardly in these days of turbulence, decay and decline.

---

6   TN: What Is the Political?

René Thom and the Theory of Catastrophes

But how does this notion of the political hinge on the topic that concerns us today, namely the 'convergence of catastrophes'? Faye is the youngest link in an entire chain that links Clausewitz to Schmitt, Schmitt to Capitant, Capitant to Freund and Freund to himself and his friends. His elders have left us and are thus not experiencing the era that we are facing today. Other crucial questions arise, including this one, to which Guillaume Corvus' book does indeed respond:

> Is the (people-killing) system capable of confronting and dealing with a large-scale catastrophe, several simultaneous or consecutive disasters over a short period of time or, worse, a convergence of several simultaneous catastrophes?

To the doctrinal corpus of Schmitt and Freund, Corvus adds that of the French mathematician and philosopher René Thom,[7] who notes that every complex system is inherently fragile and its fragility exacerbated whenever its complexity increases. Corvus exploits Thom's work insofar as it highlights the fact that a harmless event can indeed create, under the right circumstances, chain reactions that lead to an implosion- or explosion-based catastrophe. We are all familiar with this model, one that has been proposed on numerous occasions by certain climatologists and observers of natural disasters: the flapping of a butterfly's wings in Hawaii may trigger a tidal wave in Japan or the Philippines. Thom's theories mostly find their practical application in the observation and prevention of stock market collapses: indeed, small variations can result in a major crisis or crash.

Corvus thus raises the question of state management — and even that of the 'global village' — at a time of ongoing globalisation. The example of the hurricane that caused floods in New Orleans at the

---

7   TN: René Frédéric Thom (2nd September, 1923–25th October, 2002) was a
     French mathematician. He established his reputation as a skilled topologist,
     shifting his focus onto aspects of what would be later be termed 'singularity
     theory' and attaining worldwide fame as the founder of 'catastrophe theory'.

end of August already proves that the American system is unable to optimally manage two emergency situations at the same time: on the one hand, the war in Iraq, which mobilises its funds and resources, and, on the other, the floods at the mouth of the Mississippi, which was to be tamed at the basin as part of the main project launched by Franklin Delano Roosevelt,[8] a project for which the latter mobilised all of America's resources in the so-called 'managerial era' (to use the words of James Burnham[9]) and for which he started the two world wars in an attempt to glean sufficient funds (following the elimination of America's German and Japanese commercial competitors) and thus achieve his objective — that of organising, from East to West, the still heterogeneous US territory. The natural disaster that struck New Orleans acts, in this regard, as an indication of an American backlash within North America itself and, even more so, as evidence of the extreme fragility characterising hyper-complex systems when subjected to multiple and simultaneous demands. As we shall soon see, this debate is still raging in today's United States.

What Would Happen to France If It Were Struck by Four or Five Simultaneous Disasters?

In France itself, the riots that erupted in the suburbs back in November 2005 demonstrated that the French system was perfectly able to deal with riots occurring in a single city, and reasonably quickly too, but not when they broke out in several cities at once. France is therefore

---

8   TN: Franklin Delano Roosevelt (30th January, 1882–12th April, 1945), often referred to as FDR, was an American statesman who served as the 32nd president of the United States, retaining this function from 1933 until his death in 1945.

9   TN: James Burnham (22nd November, 1905–28th July, 1987) was an American philosopher and political theorist. Initially an important Trotskyist activist and a notorious isolationist, he later left the Marxist camp and became a public intellectual representing the American conservative movement. His most famous book, entitled *The Managerial Revolution*, was first published in 1941 and deals with the future of capitalism.

fragile in this regard. In order to wage an indirect war against our land in accordance with the new strategies developed by the American military staff, all one has to do is cause social unrest in several cities simultaneously. The objective of such an operation may well be to paralyse our country for a certain period of time and drive it to squander a few billion euros on dealing with such riots, billions that could no longer be invested in European space projects that compete with American ones nor be spent on the modernisation of the army and military industry (the construction of an aircraft carrier, for instance). And just try to imagine a France stricken simultaneously by an outbreak of influenza (whether of the avian kind or not), thus mobilising its hospital infrastructures in a most outrageous manner; by an eruption of riots across city suburbs, as was the case in November 2005, resulting in the mobilisation of all of its police forces; by tornadoes on the Atlantic coast, as witnessed a few years ago; and by a sudden political crisis due to the unexpected death of a major political figure. There is no need to expand on things further — based on its current configuration, France is simply incapable of coping with such a convergence of catastrophes in a coherent and effective manner.

History also proves that fourteenth-century Europe suffered a similar convergence of catastrophes. The plague that ravaged it at the time led to the demise of a third of its inhabitants. This epidemic was then followed by an endemic socio-religious crisis, with successive rebellions and peasant revolts taking place in several parts of the continent. In addition to this demographic and social collapse, Europe also experienced an invasion at hands of the Ottoman forces, which set off from the small territory controlled by the Turkish leader Osman,[10] located opposite Byzantium, on the eastern shore of the Sea of Marmara. It took a whole century, and perhaps even more, for Europe to recover (and not fully, at that). More than a century after the Great Plague of

---

10 TN: Osman I was the leader of the Ottoman Turks and the founder of the Ottoman dynasty. Due to the limited historical sources dating back to his lifetime, little is known about him.

1348, Europe would lose Constantinople (in 1453), following its defeat in the Battle of Varna in 1444. In 1477, the Ottoman hordes ravaged the hinterland of Venice. It would take another two centuries for Europe to stop the Ottoman advance after the failed siege of Vienna (1683) and almost two more centuries for the last Turkish soldier to leave Europe. Europe is indeed in danger of experiencing a 'period of turmoil', just as Russia did after the days of Ivan the Terrible, a period of unpredictable length and with equally unpredictable and devastating effects that will last until the arrival of a new 'emperor' and the return of the political.

'Long War' and 'Long Emergency': the Anglo-Saxon Debate

Let us now re-situate the publication of Guillaume Corvus' *La convergence des catastrophes* in the wider context of current strategic thinking, especially the one that stirs up debates in the Anglo-Saxon world. The first interesting book to mention in this introduction was written by Philip Bobbitt[11] and entitled *The Shield of Achilles. War, Peace and the Course of History* (Penguin, Harmondsworth, 2002–2003). In it, the author mainly explains the notion of a 'long war'. In his view, such a war lasted from 1914 to the first American offensive against Iraq in 1990–1991. Current events have, however, shown that his field of observation and investigation was actually very limited: indeed, the second American attack against Iraq in 2003 proved that the first offensive was but a stage among others. Likewise, the invasion of Afghanistan, which took place two years earlier, had already demonstrated that this 'long war' was not restricted to the two world

---

11　TN: Born on 22nd July, 1948, Philip Chase Bobbitt is an American writer, academic, and solicitor. While also famous for his contribution to military strategy and constitutional law and theory, he has authored numerous books, including *Constitutional Fate: Theory of the Constitution* (1982), *The Shield of Achilles: War, Peace and the Course of History* (2002), and *Terror and Consent: The Wars for the Twenty-first Century* (2008).

wars and the cold war, but also included previous conflicts such as the Anglo-Russian wars of 1839–1842 (by means of Afghan tribes), the Crimean War, etc. Last but not least, the notion of a 'long war' allows us to ultimately realise that no war ever ends once and for all and that all current conflicts are ultimately dependent on ancient wars, some of which even date back to protohistory (as pointed out in the United States by Jared Diamond,[12] who, in his own works, mentions for example the Indonesian colonisation of West Papua as a continuation of a proto-historic Austronesian invasion; and this type of continuity has also been observed beyond the Australian-Asian space).

If we limit our field of observation to oil wars, which are nowadays raging more than ever, the period studied by Bobbitt does not fully encompass things — indeed, the first British troops arrived in Kuwait back in 1910. The international context should therefore be explored more carefully, beginning just before World War I. As demonstrated by the news one has heard during this month of January 2006, the conflict over the oil of the Fertile Crescent[13] is not over yet. Anton Zischka, who would live to be almost one hundred years old and would remain active until the very end, was one of Jean Thiriart's major sources of inspiration. He began his very long career as an author and a journalist back in 1925, at the age of twenty-five,[14] when he published a work that would subsequently be translated into French by Payot and was entitled *Ölkrieg*.[15] It dealt with a war that took place on

12   TN: Jared Mason Diamond is an American geographer, historian and anthropologist and has written several popular science books.

13   TN: The Fertile Crescent is a crescent-shaped area of the Middle East that includes modern-day Iraq, the south-eastern fringe of Turkey and the western fringes of Iran, Syria, Lebanon, Israel, Palestine, Jordan, and Egypt.

14   TN: Anton Emmerich Zischka von Trochnov (14th September, 1904–31st May, 1997) was an Austrian journalist and one of the most popular non-fiction authors of the twentieth century. Based on his date of birth, he must have been 21 years old in 1925, not 25.

15   TN: i.e. *Oil War*, which, it would seem, was actually published in 1939, when the author was 35 years old.

several continents, for Zischka had not forgotten the Chaco War[16] of South America (tintinophiles will remember *L'oreille cassée*,[17] in which a war between the fictitious San Theodoros and its equally fictitious neighbour is triggered by the desire of American oil executives to put their hands on local oil fields).

Today, following the views expressed by Zischka and (subsequently) Bobbitt regarding a 'long war', it is the American author James Howard Kunstler, who, in *The Long Emergency* (published in French by Plon editions in 2005) adopts and updates another theme that was so very dear to Zischka — that of the scientific and energy-related challenge that will inevitably be triggered by the scarcity of oil during the next few decades. In Zischka's eyes, both private and statal scientific apparatuses should have been mobilised ages ago to respond to all kinds of monopolies. From his perspective, scientists had to rally and grant their homelands and civilisational areas the necessary tools to ensure their autonomy with regard to technology, food, energy, etc. (Zischka was, in fact, a Europeanist and not a narrow-minded nationalist). This represents yet another response to Clausewitz's question and to the necessity to properly manage peoples' natural and cultural heritage. Faye himself never hesitated to call for a diversification of energy sources and nuclear rehabilitation. In his opinion, as well as that of several other thinkers, many environmentalists are actually agents of US oil executives, who intend to keep the states of the 'Americano-sphere' under their exclusive control. This argument is by no means inconsequential, especially since oil is often a greater source of pollution than nuclear energy. To Corvus, one of the major disasters that could indeed befall us in the near future is an oil crisis of unprecedented scale.

---

16   The Chaco War, which lasted from 1932 to 1935, was a military conflict between Bolivia and Paraguay, both of which sought control of the northern part of the Gran Chaco region (known in Spanish as Chaco Boreal), as the region was believed to be rich in oil.

17   TN: The Broken Ear.

The End of the American Urbanistic Model

Corvus' arguments are re-encountered in Kunstler's writings, which proves, once again, that Guillaume's book on the convergence of catastrophes is not a marginal work by any means, as some 'aggior-namento-ed' elements of the historical channel of the old 'New Right' would have you believe (just a little heads-up from me, to try and set the record straight even in some truly desperate cases; or perhaps an attempt on my part to awaken the gullible ones who still believe, or are tempted to believe, in all those evasive and unsuccessful strategies). What Kunstler predicts in the aftermath of the 'long war' theorised by Bobbitt, or, alternatively, after the long oil war described by Zischka in his early scribblings, is a 'long emergency'. He particularly describes, and in a very imaginative way at that, the collapse of American-style urbanism, foreseeing various possible and specific situations. These cities, which are now excessively large, would find it impossible to survive if oil supplies were depleted and, by way of consequence, pri-vate cars simply vanished. Kunstler explains that 80% of all modern buildings cannot remain in good working order for more than twenty years. Indeed, flat roofs are covered with ephemeral petroleum-based coatings that must constantly be renewed. It is also impossible to provide heat for and maintain supermarkets without an abundance of oil. The rapid or gradual disappearance of oil implies a complete re-development of cities, a re-development for which no plans have ever been put in place given the predominant myth of eternal progress that prohibits any and all thoughts about a potential backlash, retreat or collapse. It would no longer be possible for cities to be horizontal, as desired by today's American urbanism. They would have to be verti-calised again, but with buildings that would never exceed seven floors. One would have to revert to using traditional masonry and carpentry wood. One can readily imagine the upheavals that such a cruel re-de-velopment would bring about in the lives of millions of people, who, as feared by Corvus, might not even survive the ordeal. Just like Corvus himself, Kunstler also predicts the collapse of compulsory education for all children: schools would thus no longer be as 'overcrowded' as they are today, but would, instead, target a limited number of young people, thus giving rise to an improvement in quality, the sole positive aspect of the impending catastrophe that shall strike us.

Thierry Wolton's 'Fourth World War'

Regarding the Islamic challenge, which Faye commented on in the manner we all know, thus causing himself some hardships, it was another author, the fashionable Thierry Wolton, who, although considered 'politically correct', sounded the alarm in his turn, yet still opted for a pro-American course which, in our eyes, is not only useless but, what is worse, inconsequential. In his book entitled *La quatrième guerre mondiale*[18] (Grasset, 2005), Wolton highlights the Islamic world's trump card, its *youth bulge*, its 'demographic reserve'. This superabundance of young and inactive men, all of whom are poorly educated and quick to adopt the worst religious clichés, acts as a fighter or suicide bomber reserve. But who stands to profit from their presence? There is no such thing as a genuinely autonomous Islamic power, and enmities and hostilities pervade the Muslim world. Despite all the ranting and vociferations, no Muslim state could ever play a federative role that would unify an aggressive *umma*.[19] Only the United States has the ability to take advantage of this readily available demographic mass and move its pawns forward within the space that stretches from Egypt to India and from the Indian Ocean to the edge of the Siberian taiga. Any endeavour to unite this territorial and demographic mass will undoubtedly be an arduous one and experience several backlashes, but the United States will always have, somewhere in this vast 'Great Middle East', tens of thousands of ready-to-arm soldiers that can participate in various operations serving its interests, to

---

18   TN: The Fourth World War.

19   TN: The entire community of Muslims worldwide.

the detriment of Russia, Europe, China or India. Not to mention currently unstable Turkey, which once acted as NATO's main supplier of potential foot soldiers and was part of the short-lived Baghdad Pact,[20] concluded during the Cold War of the 1950s. The novels penned by a young writer, Burak Turna,[21] fascinate the Turkish public: they mention a Turkish war against the United States and the (oh so unfortunate) EU, followed by a Russian-Turkish alliance that shall crush the EU's armies and raise this alliance's flag over the major buildings of Vienna, Berlin and Brussels. This reshuffling of the cards is interesting to witness: the powerful movement of the 'Grey Wolves,'[22] whose members are opposed to Turkish EU membership (and, in this respect, interesting to keep track of), seems to espouse Turna's visions.

Deferred Infanticide

Let us now return to the notion of a *youth bulge*, a demographic condition enabling one to wage long wars. To our contemporaries, who have all been fooled by the eirenic delusions that have been drilled into them over the past two or three decades, using the blood of young men seems an abomination and sacrificing them on the altar of the god Mars an unspeakable horror. In Europe, however, the sacrifice of young male generations was common practice until the end of the

---

20 TN: The Central Treaty Organization (CENTO), initially known as the 'Baghdad Pact' or the Middle East Treaty Organization (METO), was a military alliance in the days of the Cold War. The main incentive that enabled the forging of this alliance, created in 1955 by Iran, Iraq, Pakistan, Turkey and the United Kingdom and dissolved in 1979, actually came from the US, which exerted great pressure in this direction and promised both military and economic aid.

21 TN: Born on 20th January, 1975 in Istanbul, Turkey, Burak Turna is a popular Turkish novelist.

22 TN: Officially known as *Ülkü Ocakları* ('Idealist Clubs/Hearths'), the Grey Wolves (Turkish: *Bozkurtlar*) are a Turkish far-right ultranationalist organisation.

Second World War. Let us therefore refrain from burying our heads in the sand, shall we? For we have not been more 'moral' in our actions than today's Islamic hotheads and those who wish to take advantage of their passion. The battle of Waterloo, which was fought fifteen kilometres from where I am penning these words, was actually a battle of very young adolescents in which one had made all the residents of the orphanages of Hanover aged twelve years or older don the uniforms of the '*Landwehr* of Luneburg'.[23] The remarkable works of French demographer Gaston Bouthoul (who was yet another thought leader held in high regard by Faye) inform us of the Roman practice of 'deferred infanticide'. When arming these legions, Rome dealt with its excess of young boys not by leaving them exposed in the vicinity of a temple or abandoning them on a hill, but by deferring what was a common practice in protohistoric and ancient societies. Every young man was entitled to a childhood and had the right to be fed before reaching adulthood, on the condition that he later became a soldier and fought from the age of seventeen to the age of thirty-seven. Survivors would then get married and settle on the land conquered by their dead comrades. The Ottoman Empire would then adopt this practice by arming the demographic surpluses of the Turkish peoples of Central Asia and the young boys of conquered Balkan territories (the Janissaries).[24] The economic reasons behind this practice were rooted in the conquest of lands, the enlargement of the *Ager Romanus*[25] and the elimination of unnecessary mouths. The demographic blowback in Europe, as part

---

23 TN: The Luneburg Battalion.

24 TN: The Janissaries (Ottoman Turkish: yeñiçeri, meaning 'new soldier') were elite infantry units that formed the Ottoman Sultan's household troops, bodyguards and the first modern standing army in Europe. They began as an elite slave corps comprising young Christian Serbs, Greeks, Armenians, Bulgarians, and Albanians who were kidnapped and forcibly converted to Islam.

25 TN: The expression *Ager Romanus* (literally 'the field of Rome', i.e. 'the territory of Rome') was used in reference to the geographical area that surrounded the city of Rome and was inhabited by actual Romans. In this respect, it was distinct from the *Ager Peregrinus*, i.e. the 'foreign territory'.

of which paid abortion has replaced Bouthoul's deferred infanticide, has rendered this practice impossible, all at the expense of territorial expansion. As for the Islamic *youth bulge*, it shall give rise to new Turkish janissary units (if Turna's wishes ever come true), fuel Saudi *jihad* or beget a reverse janissary corps in the service of America.

What Are We to Do?

In no way should the statement of all these frightening facts, which are now *ante portas*,[26] lead to pessimism in terms of action. The responses that Europe can still bring forth in an *in-extremis*[27] surge of energy (of which it has often been capable, as demonstrated by the few Cantabrian squadrons of Visigothic peasants who defeated the Moorish victors and stopped their advance once and for all, thus initiating the *reconquista*; by the Spartans in the Battle of Thermopylae;[28] by the defenders of Vienna gathered around Count Starhemberg;[29]

---

26 TN: Literally 'before the gates', meaning 'in sight'.

27 TN: In the final moments preceding death.

28 TN: The Battle of Thermopylae is a now legendary military conflict between an alliance of Greek city-states led by King Leonidas I of Sparta, on the one hand, and the Achaemenid Empire of Xerxes I on the other. In the middle of the year 480 BC, a Greek force of approximately 7,000 men (by today's estimates) marched north to block the narrow coastal pass of Thermopylae and prevent the invading armies (which, according to scholars, comprised a total of 100,000 to 150,000 men) from entering Greece. The heroicness and tactical brilliance displayed by this small Greek army is truly the stuff of legend, and rightfully so.

29 TN: Count Ernst Rüdiger von Starhemberg (12th January, 1638–4th January, 1701) was the military governor of Vienna from 1680 and the city's defender during the Battle of Vienna (1683), a battle in which King Jan Sobieski III of Poland launched the decisive attack against the invading Muslim (Ottoman) army, thus preventing, according to many experts, the conquest of Europe in its entirety.

the one hundred and thirty-five English and Welsh soldiers of Rorke's Drift;[30] etc.) are the following:

- Faced with this *youth bulge*, one must achieve technological superiority, as was the case in proto-history with the domestication of the horse and the invention of the drawn chariot. In order to revive this 'horse master' tradition, school discipline must be reinstated, especially on a scientific and technical level;

- One must re-summon the strategic audacity of the European mind, as highlighted by the American military historian Hanson in *Why the West always won*.[31] This implies knowledge of both ancient and modern models of this intrepid audacity and the creation of a warlike, 'quiritary'[32] mythology based on real facts, as exemplified by the Illiad;

- One must reject the current dominant ideology, create a European or even Euro-Siberian (Nye) *soft power*, mock media 'emotionalism', resist historical amnesia, and put an end to what Philippe Muray[33] denounced in *Festivus Festivus* (Fayard, 2005) and, previously, in *Désaccord parfait*[34] ('Tel' collection, Gallimard), namely 'festive' ideology, in all its forms and harmfulness; this very same festive ideology that dominates the media, portrays itself as mankind's ultimate ideal, is irascible in its positions and has unleashed

---

30   TN: The Battle of Rorke's Drift, also known as the Defence of Rorke's Drift, was a clash that occurred during the Anglo-Zulu War. Just over 150 British and colonial servicemen defended the station against attacks mounted by an estimated 3,000 to 4,000 Zulu warriors.

31   TN: My personal research has only pointed to a book entitled *Why the West Has Won* by Victor Davis Hanson.

32   TN: When something is described as 'quiritary', it abides by Roman civil law, confers legal title, or, when it comes to property, is held by legal right or title.

33   TN: Considered a 'reactionary', Philippe Muray was a French essayist and novelist. None of his works have, alas, been translated into English.

34   TN: Perfect Disagreement.

a new Inquisition (one that both Faye and Brigitte Bardot[35] fell victim to).

Admittedly, this task is an enormous one to undertake and a gruelling metapolitical endeavour. And yet, it is still the one that we have chosen to take upon ourselves. It is also the task to which Guillaume Faye, who shall now take the floor, devoted his entire life. And it is now up to you to take up the torch. For we can only be crushed by disasters and our enemies if we throw up our hands in defeat and allow our brains to slumber.

ROBERT STEUCKERS

---

35 TN: Born on 28th September, 1934, Brigitte Anne-Marie Bardot is a former actress and singer and an animal rights activist. Back in the 1950s and 1960s, Bardot was one the most famous sex symbols and has, in recent years, caused great controversy by denouncing the uncontrolled immigration and Islamisation of France.

An Italian Essay on Guillaume Faye

Extract from Stefano Vaj's study entitled 'Per l'autodifesa etnica totale. Riflessioni su *La colonisation de l'Europe* di Guillaume Faye',[1] *published in L'Uomo Libero,*[2] *issue number 51, Milan, May 2001.*

A FRIEND OF GUILLAUME FAYE'S, Stefano Vaj is a young Milanese man who is active as an essayist in the rare free hours which his often-tedious daily job allows him to have. In the columns of the magazine *L'Uomo libero* (51st issue, May 2001), he has just published a very long text on the man who once embodied the hope of the French 'New Right' but was expelled from the movement using the most abject sort of methods. In his preface to the new Italian edition of Guillaume Faye's first book, *Le système à tuer les peuples*, Robert Steuckers, who was also forced out of the 'New Right', gave an overview of the main lines of Faye's personal thought before gradually explaining the infamous scheme that led to his ejection.

The two essays agree on many points, which, first of all, proves that the mistakes made by the 'New Right', and especially its leaders, are now being analysed, and, secondly, that time will inexorably destroy all lies, travesties, betrayals and treacheries that have punctuated the movement's history yet been concealed by the adepts of falsification.

---

1   TN: For Total Ethnic Self-Defence. Reflections on Guillaume Faye's *La colonisation de l'Europe*.

2   TN: The Free Man.

In the meantime, for the sake of transparency, it seems to us that the French public does indeed deserve to take heed of certain judicious passages included in Vaj's essay. Here they are:

At the time, [Faye's] critical remarks on the religious question and the positions espoused by G.R.E.C.E. in this field were already "strong".

It is a common occurrence [for all those who have experienced the NR/Historical Channel first hand] to note that the prefix "neo" comprised in the term "neo-paganism" ends up being gradually forgotten, so much so that one can easily see the obsession with "positivity" and "legitimation" emerging.

[...] Religion, from the pagan point of view, is what "binds a people together" or the thing that ties them to their own origins. As soon as paganism is no longer a positive religion, however, and unquestionably so, or if it displays a tragic and Zarathustrian courage and attempts, in a fully aware manner, to create original patterns and new "tables of values" that have undoubtedly drawn inspiration from the past which this paganism has chosen to adopt, yet still remain distinct from it, the quest for "legitimation" of one type or another becomes an absolutely central premise. This is actually the reason why, at regular intervals, Evolian and Guénonian traditionalists end up becoming esotericists ("Secret Tales", the King of the Mountain, the Occult Tradition, etc.), embracing Islam or some fringe varieties of Catholic or Orthodox Christianity, or, worse, falling into vaguely Masonic or New-Age types of syncretism.

In the eyes of G.R.E.C.E., as well as those of the *Völkisch* movement in the Germany of the 1930s before it, such a quest for legitimisation was, and still is, not metaphysical in nature but essentially "sociological", and leads one to value as "politically" important those few fossils of belief or popular customs for which one can put forward a hypothesis that points to their having an indigenous, pre-Christian or simply a-Christian origin (with examples that range from the "rabbit festival" to the "statuettes of bliss"), thus channelling the movement down a path of folklorisation.

Faced with all of this, it was once again Guillaume Faye who, in an important article published in *Éléments* magazine, called for the establishment of a secular, solar and postmodern type of paganism that was openly Nietzschean and clearly distinguishable from any and all obsessions with nymphs hiding behind each and every bush, as well as from the manias of "inverted Catholicism" that characterised a large number of NR elements, all of whom were far too conditioned both by the rivalry between them and by Christian denominations to be able to resist mimicking the latter.

It was a prophetic article when one considers the subsequent "evolutions" of a certain de Benoist, who, having been initially interested in empirio-criticism and Russell's[3] or Popper's[4] epistemology, paradoxically ended up engaging, after his book entitled *Comment peut-être païen?* and a Heideggerian parenthesis, in debates with Christians and Jews on issues that related to metaphysics or common values, within an essentially neo-Platonic or neo-stoic matrix. The purpose behind such debates was obviously that of bestowing the prize of moral superiority sometimes upon Seneca,[5] sometimes upon Paul of Tarsus,[6] or, better yet, to unanimously oppose secularisation (as seen, for instance, in *"L'éclipse du sacré"*).[7]

✴   ✴   ✴

3   TN: Bertrand Arthur William Russell (18th May, 1872–2nd February, 1970) was a British philosopher, logician, mathematician, historian, author, essayist, social critic, political activist, and Nobel laureate, and a self-declared liberal, socialist and pacifist.

4   TN: Sir Karl Raimund Popper (28th July, 1902–17th September, 1994) was an Austrian-born British philosopher, academic and social commentator who denounced the classical 'justificationist' notion of knowledge and sought to replace it with critical rationalism. His political views encompassed various elements rooted in major democratic political ideologies, including socialism/social democracy, libertarianism/classical liberalism and conservatism, all of which he attempted to reconcile.

5   TN: Seneca the Younger (c. 4 BC–AD 65), known simply as Seneca, was a Roman Stoic philosopher, statesman, and dramatist, and, marginally, a satirist of the Silver Age of Latin literature.

6   TN: Paul the Apostle, commonly referred to as Saint Paul and also known under the (Hebrew) name of Saul of Tarsus, was an apostle who taught the gospel of Christ to the first-century world, though he was not, in fact, one of the so-called 'twelve apostles'.

7   TN: As already mentioned, *L'éclipse du sacré*, i.e. 'The Eclipse of the Sacred', is a book written by Alain de Benoist and Thomas Molnar. Its very title reflects the authors' rejection of secularisation, as stated above.

Those of our readers who wish to familiarise themselves in greater detail with the end of the (neo-rightist) dream should have a look at Robert Steuckers' new and long introduction to the second Italian edition of *Le système à tuer les peuples*, an introduction that has been added to the one which I myself wrote and which was published in the book's first edition.

Towards the end of 1986, the crisis that afflicted both G.R.E.C.E. and the NR/*Canal historique* — and had been announced by Giorgio Locchi, who had stated that 'everything that becomes fashionable ends up going out of fashion' — reached a peak of ripeness. By remaining loyal to bureaucrats ever dedicated to collecting money to remunerate staff members responsible for raising funds, funds that would subsequently be used to pay further staff whose function was, likewise, one of collecting money, and so on and so forth, those that had been the driving force behind G.R.E.C.E. at the latter's very beginning had either proceeded to confine themselves to a pure bystander role or increasingly sidelined themselves from the association's daily life (if, of course, they were not simply absorbed by the system), as part of a degeneration process that mimicked that of the Church of Scientology. Others still decided to play the National Front card and follow Le Pen, thus joining a party which, in its lean times, had been snubbed most harshly by neo-rightists and which, having reaped several successes, could now in turn afford to give the NR the cold shoulder, with the latter ultimately no longer perceived as a single whole driven by a historic or political project, but merely as a body that organised conferences and produced publications within a scope of limited ambitions.

The topics which characterised the publications originating from the neo-rightist milieu (which, in essence, meant *Élements*, *Nouvelle école* and its duplicate bearing the unfortunate title *Krisis*) gradually became less and less varied and increasingly literary. Surrendering to a kind of romantic regression back in the mid-1980s, de Benoist himself confessed to Faye that he had gradually become more and more interested in 'images' rather than 'ideas'. And in a private conversation held with us at the time, Faye would describe the opposition within the movement as one between 'non-super-humanist Germano-maniacs' and 'non-Germano-maniacal super-humanists'.

Among the many consequences of this slide, one can note an extreme tendency to adopt and overvalue the most bizarre elements and aspects of the Conservative Rrevolution, insofar as the latter can claim to be dissident and having split from fascist regimes. Another fact is that the gradual re-focusing of research efforts on topics that exhibited an essentially historical, literary and mythical character was achieved at the expense of significant sociological, technical, scientific, political and economic themes with regard to which the movement had not hesitated to espouse very original and innovative positions a few years earlier.

Faced with the increasing pressure of censorship and 'one-track thinking', the neo-rightist movement responded with a growing tendency to engage in compromises on crucial topics that remained decisive. This trend was paradoxically accompanied by a tense attitude towards secondary issues or even one of 'evasion', a fact that is difficult for the historic NR's core audience to grasp and includes, in particular, several nods to Jean-Cau-style philo-Sovietism, all of which were but bouts of oneirism that were, furthermore, quickly eliminated by historic developments. Last but not least, the ability not to become trapped in the antitheses of contemporary political debates (nationalism vs cosmopolitanism, liberalism vs socialism, in favour of abortion vs opposed to abortion, ecologism vs anti-ecologism, feminism vs anti-feminism, imperialism vs anti-colonialism, communism vs anti-communism, etc.) and to contrast them with matters that are both original and unique to the NR actually gave way to an inability to take a stand on the central issues of our age or, alternatively, to a taste for glossy formulations or slogans that lack any further purpose beyond themselves.

Let us now go over the mistakes that have been made in the fields of politics and propaganda with a fine-tooth comb. First and foremost, there's the obsession with being perceived as a kind of 'black International', paired with a complete misunderstanding of the potentialities characterising a genuinely international dimension, although such an endeavour would have been perfectly possible — indeed, such a dimension would, for example, have granted the movement the capacity to overcome contingent local crises and to reduce vulnerability in the face of potential repression and media blackout. And the movement could, last but not least, have given itself the possibility to trigger the mythical mobilisation of its own militants. Secondly, the gradual emptying of G.R.E.C.E.'s central staff positions took a heavy toll, with the movement gradually falling prey to the above-mentioned micro-Leninism characterising its own officials, a micro-Leninism whose impact became increasingly suffocating in its attempt to outlive itself within the framework of its metapolitical unproductivity. This emptying process and refusal to embrace internationalisation prevented the creation of a 'current' or a 'community' whose limits and identity need not be restricted at all, as it is better to act if one is to create and maintain the richness, variety and uniqueness that typifies great cultural movements and civilisational groundswells. And what internationalisation would have made possible was, above all, the ability to avoid reaction-related shocks, penetrate the nerve centres of cultural power with greater ease and avoid this appalling 'transformation into a sect'. In the end, this ambiguity in the face of the problems of *realpolitik* ended up becoming unbearable to many, even if the NR's leadership had every right to consider these problems to be inessential; but because of a certain 'naïve idealism', 'neutrality' and 'affectedness', this disinterest ended up becoming a source of negative conditioning for all the public positions espoused by Alain de Benoist, a man who, under the auspices of Maurizio Cabona,[8] had not hesitated, back in

---

8   TN: Born on 5th September, 1951, Maurizio Cabona is a journalist and (apparently) an author as well.

the 1970s, to take charge of a column in Giorgio Pisani[9]'s *Candido*, a newspaper whose contents were not quite peaceable in essence. Guillaume Faye could not remedy this involution all by himself. He constantly undertook ever more personal and 'parallel' initiatives, ranging from the postmodern radio programme '*Avant-Guerre*' to the creation of (ephemeral) structures such as the 'European Institute of Arts and Letters' or the 'Reflection Collective on the Contemporary World', all of which were initiatives whose weight Faye was alone to bear, never receiving a penny's worth of salary for them nor any moral support or one-time funding. These praiseworthy initiatives, which, it must be said, were of great intellectual quality, were initially looked upon with indifference, with complacency, and then gradually targeted with the growing hostility displayed by the movement's leaders, who, in the event that they were not busy dealing with accounting matters, were apparently more interested in the vicissitudes of modern art, in the poetry of the elves in 15th-century Saxony or in the 'decisive' debates with Thomas Molnar as to whether the divine was actually expressed 'in' the world or 'through' the world.

Faye's final relinquishment thus became symbolic of the end of a whole cycle — just like Locchi's passing, who had already left the movement several years earlier, at a time when the NR had apparently reached its peak. Although it was the end of a cycle, it was also the beginning of a period of relative demobilisation, which reached across Europe and saw some elders confine themselves to traditional politics, with others having withdrawn either into their own private sphere or into comfortable local schools of thought, as part of an increasingly reduced interaction with the outside world. Without acting as

---

9   TN: Giorgio Pisanò, not Pisani (30th January, 1924–17th October, 1997), was an Italian journalist, essayist and politician who actually revived the *Candido* weekly, which had been established by Giovannino Guareschi and was no longer being published at the time. Through it, he conducted many journalistic news campaigns and ended up openly denouncing the socialist leader Giacomo Mancini.

the initiator of a scission nor attempting to take one single franc or file address with him, and never trying to 'convert' as Marco Tarchi had done, Faye withdrew into the shadows for ten whole years while G.R.E.C.E. continued to make use of his writings, without paying him any copyright fee, of course, yet still spreading gossip to whomever was willing to listen and claiming that Faye had gone mad, had had his brain fried by drugs or had been recruited by the CIA.

STEFANO VAJ

Should Guillaume Faye Be Lynched?

An article written by Pierre Maugué in defence of Guillaume Faye following the latter's second ejection from G.R.E.C.E. in May 2000 — text published in Nouvelles de Synergies européennes, issue number 46, June–July 2000.

I N A REPLETE and slumbering France, Guillaume Faye was the one to raise the alarm, never worrying about whether or not it was a suitable time to do so, whether he risked interrupting idle chatter and academic speeches, or whether or not the sound of the alarm bells was likely to displease those whose ears were more accustomed to Bach's cantatas or Beethoven's quartets. The sermonisers had a field day. Should one sound the alarm at a time when the fire is restricted to the suburbs, when fashionable districts remain out of harm's way and considerable numbers of firefighters protect governmental palaces?

What does one reproach Guillaume Faye for, then? One blames him for having dared to loudly and bluntly reveal, in *La colonisation de l'Europe*, an inconvenient truth that one would have liked to conceal. One fears the fact that people's awareness of what is happening in both France and Europe could, under popular pressure (as long as there still *is* a people, of course), lead to a harrowing reviewing of the policy that has now been pursued for decades on end. And no one wants that, because the policy of the ostrich has now become the

rallying point of the plural/broad Left[1] and what has become known as
the opposition.

A Provocative Book

The fact that Guillaume Faye allowed himself to get carried away by
his own words and sometimes lacked moderation is something that
we are all willing to admit. Such is the characteristic of prophets, and
all one has to do is read, or re-read, Jeremiah's imprecations to be convinced of it. But regardless of the blunders, the detail-related errors
and the expressions likely to fall foul of the law, the picture he paints
is an impressive one and cannot fail to attract the attention of all those
that are concerned about the fate of France and Europe. And yet, not
only has Alain de Benoist and Charles Champetier's New Right never
tackled the problem of immigration and Islamisation head on, offering no solution worthy of the challenges that will have to be met one
day, but it has actually found no better activity for itself than to pillory
Faye! What is the reason for such an attitude, you might ask? Was it
the desire never to be confused with political currents that are labelled
as populistic? Was it their anxiousness to present the high priests of
the dominant ideology with evidence of good conduct, so as not to
be singled out again and blacklisted? That's what we would all like to
know.

As provocative as it may seem, the title of Faye's book cannot be
criticised from a semantical point of view. In its original and primary meaning, a colony is not a territory but 'a population leaving
a country to go and live in another'. As for the word 'colonisation', it
only indicates the action of populating a territory with colonists, of
creating a colony. Unless one revises dictionaries, which is one of the

---

1   TN: The *'gauche plurielle'* (French for 'plural Left') was a left-wing coalition that
     governed France from 1997 to 2002 and comprised the Socialist Party (*Parti
     socialiste* or PS), the French Communist Party (*Parti communiste français* or
     PCF), the Greens, the Left Radical Party (*Parti radical de gauche* or PRG), and
     the Citizens' Movement (*Mouvement des citoyens* or MDC).

favourite occupations of Marxist and crypto-Marxist regimes, one cannot criticise Guillaume Faye for calling a spade a spade, and using the word 'colonisation' to qualify the movements of populations that affect both France and Europe and whose continuation has been granted the blessing of political and religious leaders alike.

This growing immigrational phenomenon's major consequence has been the fact that Islam is now spreading across all of Europe. The shadow of the minarets is being increasingly cast upon our territory, and it really does take a naivety akin to that of a radical socialist schoolteacher to actually believe, just as Chevènement does, that the Islamic religion will integrate into the framework of the Republic's secular ideals without any difficulty. Indeed, the problem posed by the implantation of Islam is not only a religious one; it is, and will steadily become, more and more political, because the distinction between the temporal and the spiritual, which is consubstantial with the history of European culture, is essentially foreign to the Islamic mindset.

Europe Has Laid Its Own Foundations by Resisting Islamic Expansionism

For fourteen centuries, Europe has laid its own foundations by constantly having to defend itself against Islamic expansionism. The most important dates of this struggle were formerly known to anyone holding academic qualifications: 732 AD, when the Frankish statesman Charles Martel stopped the Arabs dead in their tracks[2] at Poitiers; the *Reconquista* of Spain, which, having begun in the middle of the 8th century AD, did not come to an end until 1501 AD; the Turkish conquest of Constantinople in 1453; the conquering of Athens in 1456 AD, followed by the subjugation of Greece and the entire Balkans; the Siege of Vienna by the Muslim Turks in 1693, with the imperial city owing

---

2   TN: Quite literally, I might add.

its very salvation to the troops led by Charles of Lorraine[3] and Jan III Sobieski. In the nineteenth century, all of Europe was gripped by a fiery passion for liberating Greece from the Turkish yoke, a situation that acted as a prelude to the reconquest of the Balkans.[4] Delacroix would subsequently depict the Chios massacre[5] in some of his paintings; and as for Victor Hugo,[6] he would write his famous verses illustrating the Greek resistance, stating: "*'Friend,'* says the Greek child, the blue-eyed child, *"what I want from you is gunpowder and bullets."*"

A Europe That Has Lost Its Memory

Today, however, Europe finds itself afflicted with memory loss and is helping the Americans to create Muslim states in the Balkans, thus facilitating the return of Turkish influence to the region, while also accepting the establishment of increasingly larger Muslim colonies

---

3   TN: Charles V, Duke of Lorraine and Bar (3rd April, 1643–18th April, 1690) was born in exile in Vienna. He dedicated his military career to serving the Habsburg Monarchy and played a decisive part in the 1683–1696 Turkish War, which reasserted Habsburg power over South-East Europe. It is thus important not to confuse him with other men that bore the same name.

4   TN: Ferdinand Victor Eugène Delacroix (26th April, 1798–13th August, 1863) was a French Romantic artist, who, from the beginning of his career, was considered the leader of the French Romantic school. His depiction of the massacre at Chios shows sick, dying Greek civilians on the point of being slaughtered by the Turks and is, in fact, one of several paintings he produced on the topic of this very tragic event.

5   TN: The Chios island massacre involved the slaughtering of tens of thousands of Greeks by Ottoman troops during the Greek War of Independence in 1822. Greeks from neighbouring islands had previously come to urge the Chians to participate in their uprising. In reaction to this, the Ottomans landed on the island and slaughtered countless (Christian) Greeks, thus giving rise to international outrage and cultivating increasing worldwide support for the Greek cause.

6   TN: Victor Marie Hugo (28th February, 1802–22nd May, 1885) is an internationally acclaimed French poet, novelist and dramatist of the Romantic movement. He is rightfully regarded as one of the greatest French authors.

on European soil—all of this against the backdrop of unprecedented European demographic decline.

Guillaume Faye says things without treating them with kid gloves, and although he does resort to intentional provocation at times, he, at least, has the courage to state facts that others attempt to conceal and is bold enough to start debates which everyone would gladly try to avoid. In besieged Constantinople, more than five centuries ago, the local clerics chose to discuss the sex of the angels rather than encourage people to prepare themselves to defend the city; and none could ever accuse Faye of having followed their example!

Guénon Left Europe

In no way are we trying to deny the greatness of Muslim culture and that of the Arab and Ottoman civilisation; but if Europe may indeed have benefited from the exchanges that it engaged in with this 'other world', it was at a time when it acted as its own master and was not being subjected to a wave of growing Islamisation on its own territory. An example to ponder is that of René Guénon. Having converted to Islam, the only religion in which he was able to find the esoteric path he was looking for, Guénon[7] left France for Egypt. His conversion was indeed a purely personal process and he did not think he could fully live his life as a Muslim within the framework of a European society. Convinced that each and every civilisation and culture have their own path to follow, Guénon never considered the possibility that France could ever be Islamised. In his eyes, if France were to ever rediscover the path of spirituality, it would only be traditional Catholicism, the very same one that flourished until the dawn of the fourteenth century, which would act as its vector. And he was of the opinion that

---

7   AN: René Guénon initially sought to find his own path through Hinduism and published some significant works on the topic. For details, see my study entitled *L'idéologie trifonctionnelle dans l'œuvre de René Guénon* [TN: The Trifunctional Ideology in the Work of René Guénon], published in 1995 as part of the *Nouvelle école* issue dedicated to the subject of Tradition.

all subsisting aspects of European paganism, especially the Celtic one, had actually been incorporated by Catholicism.[8]

The very fact that today's neo-rightist leaders, who claim to be neo-pagan, display visible predilections for Islam — whose monotheism is the most intransigent of all — can only conjure up a smile. Indeed, although Jews and Christians are not to be shunned in the eyes of the Prophet,[9] since those of them who believe in God and have practiced virtuousness will be free of all fear and affliction on Judgment Day[10] (Sura 5:73), the same cannot be said of the pagans: *'Surely Allah does not forgive that anything should be associated with Him, and forgives what is besides that to whomsoever He pleases; and whoever associates anything with Allah, he devises indeed a great sin'.* (Sura 4:51[11]). Christianity itself is, moreover, suspected of paganism by Islam, since the latter considers the Holy Trinity to be contrary to one's belief in a single God and regards the Messiah as merely an apostle: *'They do blaspheme who say "Allah is one of three in a Trinity": for there is no god except One Allah. If they desist not from their word (of blasphemy), verily a grievous penalty will befall the blasphemers among them'.* (Sura 5:77[12]).

---

8   AN: In his preface to *Chemin de Paradis* [TN: Path to Paradise], Charles Maurras writes: *'The chain of ideas which I am putting forward is sufficiently pagan, and Christian enough, to deserve the beautiful labelling "Catholic", thus belonging to the religion into which we were born'.*

9   AN: In anticipation of the Last Judgment, rubbing shoulders with Christians is, however, inadvisable: *'O you who have believed, do not take the Jews and the Christians as allies. They are [in fact] allies of one another. And whoever is an ally to them among you — then indeed, he is [one] of them. Indeed, Allah guides not the wrongdoing people'.* (Sura V, 51).

10 TN: Based on that sura, it would seem that only the fact of embracing Islam is synonymous with believing in 'God' and practicing 'virtuousness'.

11 TN: 4:48, actually.

12 TN: 5:73.

Six Months in Dubai, Six Months in New York

Perceiving the Muslim world as an ally against US-centred globalism is another sign of naïveté. The elites of the countries of the Arabian Peninsula, who have all the financial means they could ever require, are very skilled at reconciling (the most pleasant aspects of) their traditional lifestyle with the American way of life. It is perfectly possible to live six months in Dubai and six months in New York while handling the most large-scale business affairs (I have personally seen an example of this). The dispute between the Arab world and the United States is mainly due to the Israeli problem and does not in any way reflect a principled opposition to globalism, which is perfectly in line with the ideology of Islam. The case of Iraq is an atypical one and deserves a study of its own.

As for communitarianism, it embodies the irenic ideology of a failing society. One refuses to acknowledge the fact that the balance of power between communities will always be a decisive factor and, given the current demographic situation, can only evolve to the detriment of the French. France is as rich as it has ever been, yet it is old and sickly and pervaded by a suicidal ideology. The south of the country is inhabited by young populations characterised by soaring demographic rates and fascinated by the opulence of a world that lies within reach.

Huntington's Lesson

The very notion that the economic prosperity of our regions can indeed serve as an integration factor and keep major conflicts at bay is a plausible one. There are none, however, who can predict the future, and Muslim immigration could also act as a time bomb. Under such circumstances, all those sorcerer's apprentices who have been toying with the fates of both France and Europe will feel, as always, that they should not be held accountable for their actions.

More realistic than Fukuyama,[13] Huntington[14] drew the lines along which he believed future conflicts might break out, lines that are of an ethno-cultural and religious nature. What is also clear is that, across the entire planet, conflicts of exceptional violence have been occurring along the borders of the Muslim world, regardless of whether the latter interacts with Catholic, Orthodox, Coptic, Hindu or animist populations. And how can one fail to see a connection between what is happening in Chechnya, Bosnia and Kosovo, on the very borders of the Slavic and Orthodox world?

The die is cast! The debate is now open, and even if we do not share all of his analyses and assertions, we are grateful to Guillaume Faye for having sounded the alarm. And in no way will we ever participate in his lynching!

Pierre Maugué

---

13   TN: Born on 27th October, 1952, Yoshihiro Francis Fukuyama is an American political scientist, political economist and author. He is most famous for having written a book entitled *The End of History and the Last Man* (1992), in which he alleged that the worldwide spread of liberal democracies, the free-market capitalism of the West and the latter's lifestyle may well end up bringing mankind's sociocultural evolution to an end (thus triggering 'the end of history'). In all fairness to Fukuyama, I must point out that he did amend his position at a later point when he admitted that culture could not be entirely separated from economics.

14   TN: Samuel Phillips Huntington (18th April, 1927–24th December, 2008) was an American political scientist, adviser and academic whose 1993 theory of a 'clash of civilisations' stipulated that future wars would no longer be conflicts between countries, but would, instead, involve cultures, specifying in the process that the greatest threat to world peace would come from Islam.

Guillaume Faye
(1949–2019)
Drawing by: Éric Heidenkopf

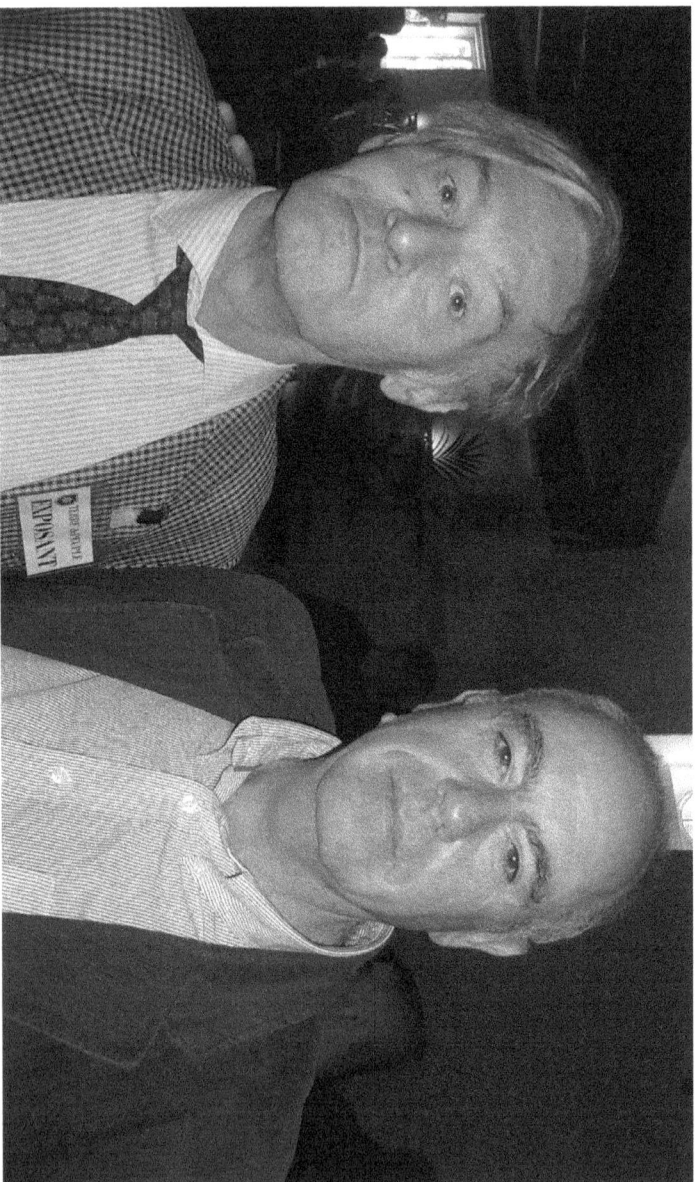

Guillaume Faye in the company of Pierre-Émile Blairon during the 11th *Terre et Peuple* round-table discussion in 2006. (Blairon private collection)

Guillaume Faye in the company of Pierre Krebs during the 11th *Terre et Peuple* round-table discussion in 2006. (Blairon private collection)

Guillaume in a brasserie in Metz on 30th March, 2012, after giving a lecture for the *Cercle Hermès* on the occasion of the publication of his book *Sexe et dévoiement*. (Dufresne private collection)

OTHER BOOKS PUBLISHED BY ARKTOS

OTHER BOOKS PUBLISHED BY ARKTOS

OTHER BOOKS PUBLISHED BY ARKTOS

OTHER BOOKS PUBLISHED BY ARKTOS

www.ingramcontent.com/pod-product-compliance
Lightning Source LLC
Chambersburg PA
CBHW021359090426
42742CB00009B/924